TulipTree Review

SPRING 2015

issue #1

TULIPTREE
PUBLISHING, LLC

TulipTree Review

Editor in Chief / Publisher
Jennifer Top

ISBN-13: 978-0692406663
ISBN-10: 0692406662

Cover photo by John Stack IV

Cover design by TulipTree Publishing, LLC

Designed and Typeset by
TulipTree Publishing, LLC / tuliptreepub.com

Contents

Lorrie Wolfe

This Is How You Begin

You must do the thing you think you cannot do.
—Eleanor Roosevelt

when what they say is
can't won't never amount to
who do you think you—

stand, pick up your wounded pen
they can't pay you enough
to make you stop

you lose track of time
you would do this anyway
this thing you can't not do

it has a life all its own
it thrums
wakes you in the night
with a ring
the Operator speaks
it's always collect

you take the call

How to Eat an Iceberg

Start at the tip
greet what can be seen
adopt an omnivorous pose
and begin

Most of what must be gnawed
lies below
you'll have to get your face down
into the cold
feel the ice burn your cheeks
sear your lungs with salt water

Adopt the form of a seal
learn to love the liquid and its harder twin
slap and slide your own smoothness
over its polished curves
keep your warm heart inside
where ice can't reach

Bore a test-hole
into the core of the ice
Seed a single atom deep, set to blow
when it explodes
let it shred off your seal-skin,

Then you can rise, like a Selkie
kiss the water farewell
and walk on the legs you have earned

Flash Fiction

Mitchell Krockmalnik Grabois

Reply

Leonard Bernstein said,

This will be our reply to violence, to make music more intensely than ever before.

So after I heard about the murder of twenty children in their Crayola classroom, I descended the splintery stairs to my cellar and sat behind my drums and beat them. By the time the other members of my band showed up, the bassist, who works as a bartender, the guitarist, whose girlfriend went back to Arkansas, and the lead singer, dark as a gypsy, I was frothed, my black t-shirt soaked with sweat, my arms pumped like a bodybuilder's, the Mounds of Venus at the base of my thumbs hard as walnuts.

My dog, who I'd saved from the pound and normally likes rock music, cowered behind the water heater, as if the shooter of children were in the room with his assault rifle. I got up to give him a lamb treat and smooth his ears back and tell him that everything was going to be all right.

The next day I took my kids to the beach. The beach attendant wore a long-sleeve, electric blue shirt, took a pull off his can of Red Bull, set it on a fence rail, grunted and grimaced as he clean-and-jerked four grungy lounge chairs, and carried them over his head down the beach.

The sun sparkled silver on an Atlantic dull as wash water. The dredge boat a hundred yards out exhaled wispy black smoke, twenty truckloads of sand in its belly. The beach was ten feet higher than it was the day before, with sand from eighty feet below the surface of the sea.

My kids complained. They'd dug deep holes, but had found no treasure here on the Treasure Coast.

Adam J. Sedia

The Fireflies

Dusk falls, shade fast engulfs the land.
The air lies calm; the night, serene.

It comes alive with lambent sparks,
Dimly glowing in ghostly green.

Each preternatural flicker marks
A life, a creature's mortal bounds.

Thronging numberless as the stars,
They flit and float in mystic rounds.

They light their own paths, just as ours
Remain unlit, unseen, unknown,

For our lights shine but inwardly,
Unnoticed even by our own.

The stars shine, too, as heavenly
Reflections of the fireflies' light:

Their fearsome flames blaze bright, expand,
And die when sapped of flagging might.

Jack Matthews

Me & Jules

Jules wasn't on his game that day. He'd already broken three dozen eggs and kept putting canned goods on top of the produce. And Mrs. McHenry does *not* like her canned goods on her produce. But you couldn't blame him; the Marietta Maid—a strawberry blonde angel with powder blue eyes—was in the store. Dressed in a red miniskirt revealing a breathtaking pair of legs long enough to reach all the way down to her black patent leather heels, she stood in aisle 3 giving out samples of French vanilla and Rocky Road. The skies were clear on that mid-July Saturday afternoon as the thermometer nudged 90° and a half gallon of brain-freezing strawberry decadence could be had for a mere 89¢ (with a coupon clipped from the *Post-Gazette*, of course). The ice cream and Double-Up Green Stamp Saturday attracted throngs of people to Fernie's Lincoln Road Market where Jules and I worked as boxboys during the summer before our senior year.

During my first break of the afternoon I sat on an overturned milk crate out back on the loading dock eating from a jar of Blueberry Buckle baby food—not McQueen-cool of course, but cheap. Although I was flush with cash, taking home the extravagant sum of $75 a week, I had better things to spend my money on than cream-filled Bismarcks.

As I spooned a bit of purple gruel from the jar, Jules, holding a pastry in one hand and a bottle of Nesbitt's in the other, pushed his way ass-end first through the screen door from the store room. He deftly kicked over another empty milk crate and sat down beside me in the shade. With his square jaw and perpetual smile, Jules reminded me of a skinny, sandy-haired Cary Grant. The similarities ended there though; Jules wore Coke-bottle-thick glasses and was painfully shy around girls.

Jules had moved into town during the sixth grade and sat in front of me in Mr. Wilterdink's class. I remember Jules' first day. He was a half-foot taller than anyone else in class and wasn't wearing any glasses when Mr. Wilterdink introduced him. The boys sat in silent awe, eyeing the newest first dibs for the lunchtime basketball game, and the girls were dumbstruck by his movie-star looks. First impressions *are* important, but they eventually wither under the ruthless scrutiny of familiarity. In spite of his appearance, Jules was a remarkably unskilled athlete and had a quiet, insecure nature. While similarly endowed athletically, I was what we used to call a wiseacre, rarely allowing my brain to control my mouth. In short, I was bully-bait.

Jules and I started hanging out and a symbiotic relationship developed between us. Because of his size, Jules deflected the bullying and, for better or worse, I guided Jules in his moments of indecision.

The next year in Mrs. Nelson's seventh grade English class, Jules—his real name was Glenn—surprised all of us with a well-rehearsed oral book report on *Twenty Thousand Leagues Under the Sea.* It was not so much book report as passionate reenactment in character and costume of Captain Nemo. And it was good. Shy and reserved in real life, in front of an audience, a switch turned and he became someone else. He earned the name Jules that day and it stuck.

As Jules lowered his butt onto the milk crate, he took a swig from his soda and said, "Man-o-man, what a zoo in there."

I shifted my weight and took another bite of Blueberry Buckle. "So, are you going to ask her out?" I asked.

"Who?" Jules looked down at his shoes and blushed.

"Don't play coy with me, Buster Brown. You detour down past the ice cream freezer on every price check and little Miss Marietta Maid is on you like paisley on a hippie." In a piercing falsetto I mocked, "Oh, Jules . . . I need some more Rocky Road down here . . . Jules, sweetie, can you tell the dairy guy I need more chocolate?"

Then back in a normal voice, "What are you going to do about it?"

"Nothing, probably," Jules responded. "She's gotta be a college girl—must be at least twenty, maybe twenty-five."

"Holy crap!" I said. "You really don't know who that is?"

"Should I?"

"That's April Armstrong, cheerleader and senior class treasurer at East High. She was even Homecoming Queen last year."

"How do you know?"

"Cuz, I know everything, numbnuts." Truth be told, I had seen Bob Hipsmann in the parking lot earlier in the day and Bob (the most McQueen-cool kid I ever knew) really did know everything. He pooped the scoop on April— although I made up the Homecoming Queen part.

"Cheerleader? Homecoming Queen? Well that settles that," Jules said. "She'd never go out with me. No sense in asking."

"Are you NUTS?!" I asked. "This is the chance of a lifetime. If you don't take a shot at this, you'll regret it. I don't know why, but she seems to like you." I lied again. Lots of girls were attracted to Jules' *aw-shucks* awkwardness and good looks behind those gawd-awful glasses, but he'd never worked up enough courage to go out on a real date. Oh sure, on most Saturday nights after work we'd go down to Chuck and Mabel's Pizza Bowl with the Huntington Twins, Margaret and Cathy; but sharing a large pepperoni and three lines of bowling doesn't count as a date. Besides, we'd all been in Mr. Wilterdink's class together so Margaret and Cathy weren't really girls, just friends.

Jules, Margaret, Cathy, Bob, and I all attended Lincoln Road High School on the west end of town, ten blocks south of Fernie's Market. In the topography of high school social circles, we were positioned in white space between circles—not smart enough to be brainiacs, not musical, certainly not jocks, not FFA or ROTC, not anything really. McQueen-cool Bob, with California-blonde hair grown down around his collar and remarkably mature facial hair, was a little different. While the rest of us were part of the invisible white space, Bob occupied a uniquely visible position in that space. He had the uncommon ability to talk to anyone about anything, anytime, belonging to no circle and every circle at once. A loner never alone, everyone considered Bob a friend. It didn't hurt that he drove (and could fix) a testosterone-laced '64 El Camino with a 327 short-block V8 and dual exhausts.

"Bob thinks you ought to ask her out," I told Jules.

"Yeah, right. How would he know and why would he care?"

"He was in the store this morning picking up a box of Cocoa Krispies. He saw you back by the dairy case getting a dozen eggs to replace the ones you dropped. He told me April was flirting with you."

A flash of uncertainty crossed Jules' face. "Does he think I'd have a chance?"

"He talked to her after you rushed back up front. She thinks you're cute." I'm such a liar. I hate myself sometimes, but this was important. Jules had a shot at this. He was tall and handsome even with the glasses, and for all April knew he could have been the coolest cat at Lincoln Road. And if it worked out, she surely had a friend or two over there at East High who wouldn't mind going out with "a *really* nice guy" on a double date.

Jules blushed again and appeared to stop breathing. "What do you think I should do?"

Using a wooden ice cream spoon, I catapulted my last blob of Blueberry Buckle toward Jules and caught him square on the forehead. "Gawd, you're such a numbnuts," I said (this was my "numbnuts" year). "If Bob thinks you should ask her out, what more do you need?"

Jules wiped the baby food off of his head, shrugged, and stared off into the distance without making any promises.

* * *

As usual the Pizza Bowl was awash with the persistent clatter of pins falling and the sweet-tingly smell of stale beer and cigarette smoke. Margaret, Cathy, and I were already into the third frame of our first game when we saw Jules at the counter checking out a pair of shoes and choosing a ball. I had left him behind at Fernie's Market after closing up with instructions not to show his pasty-white face down here unless he managed to ask April out. He'd made whiney excuses all afternoon: "too many people around," "she's busy," "might have a bugger in my nose" . . .

"All right," I had said, "the store is closing, she's taking apart the Marietta Dairy display and cleaning up—you go to the john, check the mirror for buggers, and then ask her out before she gets away."

"What should I say? Where would we go?"

"Keep it simple. Just ask her if she wants to see a movie next week. That new Steve McQueen flick is playing down at the drive-in. When you're finished up here, I'll be down at the bowling alley with Margaret and Cathy. Meet you there."

As Jules approached—bowling ball cradled in one hand, shoes dangling from the other—I couldn't read the look on his face. He put the ball on the return rack, sat down without a word, and started taking off his street shoes. I pulled my glasses down my nose and took direct aim. "I've told the girls what's going on, numbnuts, so fess up. What happened?"

"Okay," he whispered as a broad smile crossed his face, "next Saturday we're going to the Beastly Burger and then over to the Vision Quest Drive-In to see *Bulitt*."

"Well done, Captain Nemo," I shouted. "One extra-large Double Pepperoni Deluxe coming up. My treat!"

Cathy flashed a weak smile as she sat back and gamely gave Jules a thumbs-up. Margaret scrunched her lips, looked at me, but addressed Jules tartly, "Fine, now bowl, you moron. You're three frames behind." The twins were not identical, but both had deep brown eyes—almost black—and sported wavy chestnut hairdos. Margaret was taller with bigger bones and a shorter temper. Cathy, easy going and smartest of our group, was the only reason we had all passed chemistry the previous year.

I had winced a little at the girls' reaction when earlier, before Jules arrived, I told them I'd goaded Jules into asking April out. "What do you mean, 'bad idea'?" I asked, offended at the suggestion.

"You know Jules. He'd step in front of a train for any of us, but naïve as a polliwog in a shark tank." Cathy responded. "A girl like April will eat. him. alive."

"What do you mean by that, 'A girl like April'? You don't know her," I said.

"Yeah, well, I know the type. She's a cheerleader, probably dating half the football team, and goes through more boyfriends in a month than cans of hairspray. If she does go out with him, it will be because he's cute. She might even go out with him a few times—she's blonde, after all. Might take her a while to figure him out. But sooner or later she'll find out he's just one of us geckos and switch brands— hairspray, boyfriend, all about the same to a girl like her. Jules isn't ready for that."

Margaret, being Margaret, was downright belligerent. "Cathy's right. And that makes you one giant asshole. You should stay out of this and let Jules find his own way." Margaret had me dead to rights on being the asshole. I was okay with occupying that niche but sometimes overplayed the part.

"But Jules just needs a little shove," I said. "Even if it's just one date with April, think of the rep he'll have when school starts. Me and Jules walkin' around the halls of Lincoln next year—we'll be like Studley Whiplash and Cool McQueen."

"Prick," Margaret retorted. "As usual, it's all about you. A little shove? Hope it's not off a cliff. If it's a matter of 'rep' why don't *you* ask her out?"

"Right. A fat, curly-headed, red dwarf like me? She'd laugh in my face. At least Jules has a chance." Truth was, I had never been on a real date either, but Jules was ready. I wasn't. In spite of his shyness, he had good looks, and something else—stage presence? charisma? moxie? Whatever, he had it. I, on the other hand, was born ugly and puberty had only made things worse. I wouldn't be ready until I got the acne under control.

But Margaret was getting close to another truth. Unconsciously I wanted Jules to be my proxy to cool. Fat, ugly, face full of zits—none of that mattered if your best friend was Studley Whiplash. You got a free ticket to the cool-kids' tent. Beginning to recognize how I was using Jules, I felt a speck of heartburn grow into a nauseous wave of guilt.

"Okay," I said, "maybe he'll chicken out, maybe she'll say no, but the deed is done. If he asks, and she says yes, let's not piss in his cherry Coke for now." We finished shoeing up and I bowled first. A gutter ball.

* * *

The parking lot at Fernie's Market was still crowded with Saturday afternoon shoppers. Jules and I had talked the assistant manager into scheduling him into an earlier shift and I was going to put in some overtime after closing to restock the shelves—something Jules and I normally did during the quieter times on Saturday afternoons. I was on break and Jules was taking off to get ready for his date as we traded cars.

"Here are the keys. Don't forget, it's a little tricky shifting into second, but you can go straight from first to third if you punch it." Jules had driven my car before, but I didn't want him to embarrass himself with April. Jules' orange and white '58 Nash Metropolitan—the Creamsicle—wasn't going to cut it. My midnight blue '61 Ford Falcon was only marginally better. But with a "three-on-the-tree" manual transmission, ninety-two thunderous horses under the hood, and an 8-track tape player mounted on the drivetrain hump, it was a less visible dork-mobile than Jules' car. I had wanted to ask Bob about borrowing his El Camino, but Jules would have none of that. "Besides," he said, "can you picture Bob tooling around in the Creamsicle?"

Jules took my keys and pleaded, "What will we talk about?"

"School, music, sports . . . ah, no, on second thought, not sports. Not your strong suit and she's a cheerleader. You'll think of something."

Panic clouded his face. "You'll think of something" was not a comforting thought for Jules. Thinking fast, I added, "Just play the part, but play it cool. You're Bogart, she's Bacall. She'll do most of the talking anyway; just ask her what she likes. If the conversation lags, I've got a few tapes in the back seat—Steppenwolf, Led Zeppelin, Donovan—the whole ball of wax. But *don't* pick the music, ask her to choose something."

"Should I wear my glasses? I hate my glasses. They make me feel like crap."

"*Yes*, wear the damn glasses. She knows you have them and you'll just knock something over without them." I shook my head in disbelief. How could any seventeen-year-old be so clueless?

A blue cloud of pungent smoke billowed from the end of the exhaust pipe as Jules started the Falcon and threw it into reverse. As he drove away I headed back inside the market with a sick feeling in my belly. Cathy's words reverberated through my brain: eat. him. alive.

* * *

Late Sunday morning I drove the Creamsicle over to Jules' place to exchange cars. Jules had two younger brothers and an older sister in a house with only three bedrooms, so he slept on a cot next to his dad's Oldsmobile Cutlass in the detached garage. The place smelled of gasoline and lawn fertilizer but he had organized a cozy little spot for himself with a ragged pillow, a scratchy wool Hopalong Cassidy blanket, and a trouble light for reading. I parked out front, walked around to the back, and pounded on the garage door. No answer. My Falcon was parked in the driveway so I knew he was home. I pounded harder. I heard some rustling and something fall over—a rake or a shovel or something. Finally, Jules' squinting face and rumpled blonde hair appeared in the window next to the door.

"Hey, numbnuts, time to get up," I hollered.

"Just a sec," Jules mumbled as he disappeared back into the darkness of the garage.

Finally the door opened a few inches and I pushed my way in. "So what time did you get home?" I pressed, not wanting to waste any time off-topic.

"About one, I guess."

"Out-effin'-standing. That sounds promising."

"It went okay," Jules said as an involuntary smile briefly flashed across his face.

I could tell it went better than okay. "You have to do better than that. The truth, the whole truth, and nothing but the truth, so help you Steve. All the gory details. Fess up, buddy."

"Well, you were right. She did most of the talking. We had double cheeseburgers and then went over to the drive-in. The movie didn't start until about ten, so we listened to a couple of your tapes, watched the movie, and then I drove her home. That's about it."

"Puhleeeeze. Spare me the *Reader's Digest* version. Did you kiss her?"

"I guess."

"You guess?! You're out with April Armstrong and you can't remember if you kissed her? I'll take that as a yes. Did you French?"

Jules flushed with embarrassment. "None of your beeswax, butthole." I was surprised. Butthole was a little out of Jules' wheelhouse. With some relief, I noticed the sick feeling in my belly had evaporated. April was not the shark Cathy had thought. But I knew Jules well enough to know that "butthole" meant the conversation was over, so it was time to scram.

"I brought the Creamsicle over," I said, handing him the keys.

"Thanks. Your keys are over there on the shelf. You working today?"

"Yeah. I'm working from four 'til closing. You?"

"Same. See you there." Jules lay back down on his cot. I took the hint, the keys to my Falcon, and left him to his dreams.

In the days that followed, Jules and April had a second and a third date—a sit-down dinner at Puchinni's and a Sunday picnic out at Hadley Lake. For the picnic he'd worked up the nerve to drive the Creamsicle rather than borrow my car. I was ecstatic, Jules was finally coming out of his shell and I was anticipating a truly outstanding senior year. Yet after the date up at Hadley Lake, Jules became uncharacteristically tight lipped about the details. Meanwhile, Cathy and Margaret held firm to their doubts.

"There's something not right about this," Cathy told me one afternoon. "Jules is one of us, and April is . . . well, Major League material."

We were sitting at a picnic table basking in the sun just outside the Dairy Queen across the road from Fernie's, lapping up a couple of vanilla soft-serves. Cathy had tracked me down at work and said she wanted to talk.

"What about Beauty and the Beast? Or Cinderella and the Prince? True love knows no bounds," I poetically intoned, immediately sensing the corny absurdity.

"Cut the crap. This ain't no fairy tale," Cathy griped.

"Yeah, well, what can we do? It's none of our business now."

"Margaret wants to kidnap April, tie her up in a root cellar, and feed her glass-encrusted Brussels sprouts and cod liver oil until she spills her guts. I told her that might involve prison time but she thinks it's worth the risk." Cathy shook her head. "Kidding aside," she continued, "I can't help feeling this ends badly for Jules."

"Maybe not. Sure, it may not last, but nothing lasts forever and he'll always remember the time he dated April Armstrong."

"Or suffer a lifetime of depression and regret and end up in a cardboard shelter down on Smith Street with the winos and bimbos."

After a few moments of turning that image over in my mind, I asked, "So what's the plan?"

"Margaret's crushing glass as we speak. But for now, why don't you press him a little harder—find out if he's going gorillas or just having a good time. We have a cousin over at East High. I'll see what he thinks about April."

Cathy's concern worried me. She was not only smart, but something about those brown eyes and calm demeanor made her seem wise beyond her years. I couldn't bullshit Cathy and she knew it. And, besides, I'd have been up to my alligators in eyeballs in that chemistry class without her.

* * *

Try as I might, Jules remained vague about his dates with April. I interrogated, whined, threatened, coerced, and even begged for details. No dice. The breakthrough came a week later on a withering Sunday afternoon. I was done early at Fernie's and walked to the back parking lot where employees could park in the shade of a row of ancient oak trees. I found Bob Hipsmann sitting on the hood of my Falcon, legs dangling over the grill. A shot of envy welled up in my belly seeing his El Camino backed into the parking spot next to my Falcon. Just keep saving my money, I thought.

"What's cookin', Bob?" I asked.

"Same ol' stew," Bob replied as he wiped the sweat from his forehead. "Got a few minutes?"

"Sure, what's on your mind?"

"Jules. He still dating April Armstrong?"

"Yeah, I guess. Why?"

"Happened to be up at Hadley Lake last night. Some kinda after-midnight party up there on Hunnecker's Bay. Lots of 3.2 shit and other nonsense. But I did recognize April. Looked like she was really enjoying herself with one of the guys up there, if you get my drift. You know if Jules was up there?"

Shit-kicked in the gut, I hesitated. "No, I guess not. He closed up here last night and then worked graveyard stocking shelves. Besides, doesn't sound like his kinda party."

"That's what I thought," Bob said. "You and Jules go back a long way. Better you handle it than me." Bob hopped down off the hood of my car and pulled the keys out of his jeans pocket. "Your move," he chirped with a little nod of his head as he climbed behind the wheel of the El Camino.

"Thanks, Bob," I said, sarcasm scarcely concealed. "I really appreciate this."

* * *

My first move was to call Cathy. We met the next morning on the back patio at her house. "Don't tell Jules just yet," Cathy said. "You need to confront April and see if she's willing to own up to this and then let her do the dirty work."

I hadn't slept well the night before. Recurring dreams kept waking me up—visions of a broken-down, bearded, sandy-haired bum with thick glasses shivering and huddled up in a cardboard carton. Followed by ghostly images of a gravestone inscribed, "ate. him. alive." Damn Dickens anyway.

"Wouldn't it be better for you to do this? Woman-to-woman?"

"You chicken-shit asshole, you started this. You need to finish it."

I flicked a dead leaf off the patio table in frustration. "Yeah, you're right," I said, "but how? I don't know where she lives and don't think a phone call would work."

"One step ahead of you there, Captain America. Here's her address," she said as she handed me a tattered scrap of note paper. "I got it from my cousin. Rumor is that her parents are out of town this week, that's why she was able to party all night up at the lake on Saturday. Go over there this afternoon and get it done."

"But I work until six—"

"Perfect," Cathy interrupted, "she probably doesn't get out of bed until three."

* * *

The house at 435 Martin Street was a blonde brick ranch house with dense green juniper bushes at each corner and a thick-trunked maple in the front yard. I pulled up and parked on the street in front of the house. I shut down the Falcon and took a couple of deep breaths to quell the boiling cauldron in my gut.

As I walked up the driveway, beads of sweat formed on my forehead and I could see the front door was open—not unusual on a sultry August evening. I could hear the television blaring through the screen door, a weeknight variety show we used to watch as kids called *Hullaballoo*. I distinctly remember Petula Clark was singing "Downtown."

I lightly rapped on the screen door. No sense scaring anyone, I thought. No one answered and I thought about leaving, but Cathy would have had my liver for lunch. I didn't leave. I rapped a little harder. Still no answer. I screwed up some courage and rang the doorbell.

A shadow cautiously approached the screen door. "Can I help you?" April's voice, I thought.

"April?" I asked, wanting to make sure.

April came close to the screen, cocked her head, and squinted. "And you would be?"

"Jules' best friend."

She glanced over my shoulder and saw my Falcon sitting on the street and nodded in recognition. "Ahhh, yes," she said as she opened the screen door, "I remember. You work at Fernie's Market too. You want to come in?"

I hadn't expected to be received so politely. My heart skipped a beat before I replied, "S-s-sure."

She led me into a dimly lit wood-paneled living room that smelled of old leather. The tiny flickering black-and-white image of Petula Clark swaying back and forth on the small screen took center stage. April noticed my distraction, turned the TV off, and turned on a table lamp.

"Have a seat," she said, motioning toward the couch as she squared up toward me. She made no move to sit down herself.

The room was cluttered with issues of *TV Guide*, the *Saturday Evening Post*, and *Redbook*. A half-eaten bowl of popcorn sat on the floor in front of the TV, a few kernels spilled out on the green shag carpet. She was dressed in an oversized plaid flannel shirt, denim capris, and white Keds. She wore no makeup and her long blonde hair was wildly unkempt, save for a disheveled attempt to pull it back from her face with a blue bandana. Instead of the sophisticated twenty-something image of the Marietta Maid, I saw April that evening as just another seventeen-year-old high school girl grooving out on Petula Clark.

"You want something to drink?" she asked. "I've got Coke, Tab, 7-up . . ."

"Thanks, I'm not thirsty," I said.

April shrugged and plopped down in a recliner that I assumed would be her dad's chair if he were home. We stared uneasily at each other for a long time. Finally, "So how's Jules doing?" April asked. "I miss him."

What a bitch, I thought. "He's doing okay, I guess."

"Did he send you over here?"

"Of course not. He doesn't know anything about this."

She cocked her head and looked at me quizzically. "So why are you here?"

I hesitated a moment and then said it. "I heard from someone I trust that you were up at Hadley Lake on Saturday night."

"Might have been," she replied. "What business is that of yours?"

"Jules wasn't up there with you. He was working."

"Uhhhh, okay, so what's your point?"

"My point?" I began, with anger welling up in my belly. "My point is that if you're dating one guy, you don't go up to Hadley Lake in middle of the night and make out with some other guy."

April looked confused. "Jules and I aren't dating anymore. We were, but that ended a couple of weeks ago."

"Say what?" It was my turn to look confused. "That makes no sense. He would have told me if you'd dumped him."

"Dumped him? He broke it off!" April almost laughed. "He didn't tell you? That would be just like him, I guess." She paused and glanced toward the popcorn on the floor, thoughtfully looking through the bowl at something beyond. "He was soooo sweet about it, though," she continued. "Told me how much he liked spending time with me, but thought we'd both be better off dating people from our own schools, especially with senior year coming up. Told me I could call him next summer if I wanted. But I knew. I never had a chance with Jules."

My head reeled. "Are we talking about the same Jules here? Skinny, Coke-bottle glasses? Drives an orange and white Nash?"

"Gawd yes. Dreamboat quiet and so smart! He'd just listen while I'd go chattering away about this and that." April paused and then as her face brightened, "And that *car*—the Creamsicle? How adorable is that?"

I looked around the room, half expecting Rod Serling to materialize out of the shadows, cigarette clenched between his fingers, intoning the familiar refrain, *the middle ground between light and shadow, between science and superstition. . . . This is the Twilight Zone.*

"Well," I said, trying to hide my embarrassment, "I guess my work here is done. I'd better go and have a talk with Jules."

"Say 'hi' for me."

"Will do. See ya around."

April showed me out. I got into my Falcon and drove back across town through strangely unfamiliar streets.

* * *

The next day was Tuesday, a quiet day for customers at Fernie's, but the day most of the inventory was delivered for the weekend specials. Jules and I and two other boxboys got to work a double shift, unloading trucks, rotating perishables, and restocking shelves. After facing up the dairy, I looked at my watch—time for a break. I found Jules stocking the shelves on aisle 6—baking products. He was cleaning up after snagging a bag of flour with his box cutter.

"Hey, numbnuts, it's break time," I hollered from the end of the aisle. "When you get that mess cleaned up, grab me a jar of Gerber's Banana-Pineapple. I'll get you a Nesbitt's from the cooler and meet you out back."

I was sitting on my customary milk crate with eyes closed, half dozing in the late summer heat when I heard the screen door slam. As soon as I opened my eyes I saw a baby food jar flying toward my head and caught it mid-air, narrowly averting a banana-pineapple disaster.

"A little warning next time, Jules. Please? Your drink is over there in the shade."

Jules pulled up his milk crate, sat, and pried the lid off his soda with his price stamper. "Not long now," Jules said as he raised his bottle in a toast. "A couple of weeks and we'll finally be seniors."

I'd been up most of the night thinking long and hard about how to approach Jules about this April thing. No easy way around it, so I plunged in. "So, Jules, how are things going with April?"

"Ummh, okay, I guess," Jules said as he looked down at his feet and squirmed around on his crate. "I'm thinking she's not going to want to date a gecko like me once school starts. She'll be hammered with pep rallies, football games, and dances over there at East. Wouldn't be much fun for me, either."

"Jules, look at me," I said. "I've got a confession. Bob told me he saw April having a good time up at Hadley Lake last Saturday. I thought she was tomcattin' around, so I went over to have a talk with her."

"Yeah?" Jules glanced at me sideways and ran a hand through his hair. "When did you see her?"

"Last night."

"So what'd she tell you?"

"The truth, I think. Why didn't you tell me you broke things off with her?"

"Why didn't you just come to me after you'd talked to Bob?"

"Because," I started slowly, "I didn't think you had it in you to break off with a girl like April. I thought April was a shark and you were shark bait. If she'd been foolin' around, I thought you'd end up doing something stupid. Start living on Purina products and sweet cherry wine. I thought, well, I thought a lot of things, but I guess I thought wrong." I was talking faster now, saying things I hadn't been fully conscious of before.

"Yeah, well, I guess I thought wrong too," Jules said. "I thought I wanted to date April. She's nice enough, but she doesn't even *like* Steve McQueen movies. She talks a lot but doesn't say much. I guess I asked her out because, well, I don't know, because it seemed like the thing to do. Between you and Bob, I would've felt like a warmed-over rabbit turd if I'd chickened out." Jules paused a few moments and then continued, "We aren't kids. I don't need you telling me what I should do anymore. Not your fault, I let you do it. It was easy. It was safe. We're seniors— adults now. Maybe it's time we started acting like it."

"Shit," I said as my chest tightened with a surprising mixture of panic and fear. It was my turn to squirm uncomfortably on my milk crate and look at my feet.

* * *

Pins exploded at the end of the lane as Jules bowled the first strike of the night. He turned toward us and flashed a triumphant double bird. It was the last bowling night before school started. Margaret enthusiastically thrust both fists into the air,

"YEAH! We're going to cream your asses tonight," she taunted as she shot Cathy and me a look of disdain.

"Don't get cocky, sister," Cathy said, "it's still early."

Cathy got up, reached for her ball on the return rack, and raised it to her chest as she lined up to bowl. She was dressed in her bowling ensemble—white cotton shirt and dark brown slacks. Her butt wiggled a little as she prepared to push the ball down the lane. As Jules sat down, Margaret gave him a congratulatory punch on the shoulder. Cathy's first ball felled nine pins, but she cleaned up the spare.

Then it was Margaret's turn and Cathy returned to her seat next to me. "So are you and Jules okay?" Cathy whispered to me as Jules watched Margaret bowl from the other side of the booth.

"Peas in a pod," I responded quietly with fingers crossed.

"Why didn't he tell us about breaking up with April?"

"Embarrassed, I guess. He said we'd made such a big deal about it, he thought we'd be pissed or something."

"*You* made a big deal about it," Cathy said a little louder than she intended.

"No harm done. All's well and all that shit," I said.

Satisfied, Cathy changed the subject. "You taking physics this year?"

"Physics?" I asked. "I hadn't thought about it. Are you?"

"Yeah, Dad says I should."

"Then I guess I will, if you promise to help me with the homework."

"You don't think it will hurt your rep at school, Mr. Cool McQueen?"

"Naw, Jules is my best friend. The only thing cooler than dating April Armstrong is dating and then *dumping* April Armstrong. Studley Whiplash and Cool McQueen prowling the halls of Lincoln Road High School as seniors? It'll be outstanding."

Cathy smiled at me as she shook her head and stated the obvious: "You are the biggest asshole I know."

Guy Traiber

Pension Gretel

Futile debates about smoking and god are heating up around the wooden table. Not in that order. *Leave me alone* says the loser and seals the argument, the smoker goes outside into the narrow streets of stone and wood, where the morning's chill is disturbed by an orange garbage truck. There is poetry in the streets. One man wears a brimmed hat which looks fitting to a similar town, two decades ago. There is a poetry menu standing beside him. Words are cheap today: they are thrown purposelessly around a table, rising and descending without a taste and accent. No one stops by the poetry reciter. He smiles to me and I do not understand a word he says. Back outside the room of defeat the window's glass offers shadowy art of those who choose to stay inside with the winter breakfast. The early morning sky shares pure lights that caress the ancient wooden girders of the building. It's warm inside and pleasant apart from the loser's song and the poets' grief. And I cannot find the right word to finish with.

Konstanz, 2010

It Lacks the Glory

My words don't carry
my inner rolling thunder
nor the pain and passion
caused by flesh and love.

My lines fail
        to echo
my heart beat,
they are like the peeling wall
of a modern glass building;
it lacks the glory
of pale mat colors
and the deep
proud feeling
of a worn-out rock castle.

I am rushing forward
like my generation, like the youth
of all ages,
desiring everything—
now and easy
like pulling money
from a street's wall.

My work, my self photographing,
is stained by that haste
but I am old enough too
to have the patience
and I can wait
till it burns itself out.

The Yin and the Yang of It

It was Will's first time inside the justice building. He and Cissy lived just north of Austin and didn't come downtown much. The building wasn't hard to find but he had to park three blocks away. Maybe that's what was keeping Cissy, the parking. That and the long drive. He glanced at his watch. She better hurry. Court would be starting any minute.

"So which one of you got charged?"

Will looked at the man sitting next to him. Chaz, he said his name was. The courtroom was only about a quarter full of people, but he had chosen to plant himself at Will's elbow. He sat down and began asking questions. Will didn't see any harm in answering, and Chaz twisted the end of his goatee as he listened. He was a small, dark guy with a shaved head. His black goatee was waxed into a little spike that fish-hooked forward.

"I mean, who got charged with the crime, you or your wife?"

"My wife," Will said.

"After you told her she could make one big decision for you? Why'd you do that, anyway?"

"It was just an experiment we decided to try. A couple of weeks ago. And it was a two-way agreement. My wife would make a decision for me, and I'd make one for her."

Will hadn't told him the full story, of course. It was too long and involved, and he would have needed to start with how he worked for Hazzenack's Adverdazzling. They offered "a more dynamic approach to advertising" and used all the traditional techniques, plus some that Mr. Hazzenack had developed over the years. Hazzenack was always walking past their cubicles, thumping his watermelon belly and urging them to upgrade. "Sell them what they need, and *then* some!"

Will was a good salesman and bounced in and out of the office's Stellar Seller slot. He was surprised he ever ended up on top at all, what with the kinds of accounts he handled—the Weehumpt U. Law School, The Intellectuals of El Paso Dating Service, and others. The dating job nearly turned into an international incident when a rival service across the river in Mexico complained about the El Paso company using a plural in its name.

One of his latest jobs was to promote a shopping mall. It was a small neighborhood mall that was losing business, so he convinced the storeowners to band together and hire Hazzenack's. He guaranteed the publicity campaign would generate enough new business to pay for itself.

The storeowners bought an "in-your-facetime" package, one of the more aggressive offered by Hazzenack's. The package included things like word-of-mouth seeds (planted both online and at large public gatherings), leafleting, and TV time that went beyond mere commercials. For the TV coverage they usually bribed local news crews to shoot their generic pieces with selected storefronts in the background, but Will had gone a step farther with the mall job. He'd arranged to get its candy store mentioned in a story.

The story aired the night that he and Cissy began their decision-making experiment. Will was on the couch when the late news came on and the anchorman said they would be right back with dramatic footage of a medical incident. The show went to commercial and Will started to call Cissy over to watch, but he didn't want to interrupt her. She was busy with her dollhouse display in the corner of the living room.

Will studied her as she leaned over the display. The thigh muscles of her tanned and shapely little legs strained against her tight pink shorts, and her T-shirt strained across her breasts. She still had her hourglass figure at twenty-eight, though a little more sand slipped through the choke point each year.

Will was thirty and showing some sand shift, too. He'd begun using one of the treadmills scattered around at the office. For at least a half hour each day he put on his headset telephone and talked to clients while he walked, and if he saw Mr. Hazzenack coming he would click the odometer ahead a mile. Sometimes Hazzenack stopped and checked the employees' mileage. If he approved he would give a slap on the back or a thumbs-up.

Cissy hovered over the dollhouse yard. The band of her jeweler's goggles rested tiara-like on her head, and she was using a pair of tweezers to place a small kite in the upper branches of a bonsai oak tree. The tip of her tongue stuck out between her lips in concentration.

The display always impressed Will. It sat on an elevated base next to a big window and consisted of the house and a well-tended little yard complete with stunted trees and a shoe-sized swimming pool. The grass in the yard was real. Cissy mowed it occasionally using battery-powered barber's shears. Toy lawn furniture was scattered here and there and a bonsai hedge bordered the whole thing.

When the kite was in place and Cissy straightened up Will told her his story was about to come on the news. She looked at him and the jeweler's lenses magnified her eyes. They were deep, deep green, like peepholes to some verdant land beyond her tanned and freckled face. The brown hair that framed the face was still full and wavy, but shorter now than when they first met.

"Your shopping mall thing's coming on?"

"Yeah. The actor. Let's watch together."

Cissy hung her goggles on a miniature lamppost at the corner of the display and padded over to the couch. She stretched out sideways, leaned against Will and teased open the top of his robe. His reddish chest hair was still damp from the shower he took after getting home late from work. He looked down and saw her index finger push through the hair, parting it on a course to a nipple. The fingertip circled the nipple, making it hard, and making him hard down below too, and then...

The news came on and he sat forward.

"This is it."

Cissy muttered something as the actor Will had hired began his performance.

Earlier in the evening they followed a news crew to a story, then after the crew finished, the actor staged a heart attack. He fell to the ground as he was walking past the news van. The cameraman immediately clapped his camera on him, and the reporter stuck her mic in his face and began asking questions. The actor only got offscript once, when he plugged the dinner theater where he was currently appearing, but it was a quick plug, then he went into his death scene. He clutched his chest, looked at the camera and said, "Life is short. Buy your wife a box of candy at Anhalt's Confectioneries." That was the candy store Will was promoting, from the shopping mall. The camera was zoomed in on the actor's face by then, and if you looked closely you could see the pancake makeup he'd used to achieve a heart attack pallor. He gave the candy store's address, followed by the phone number, and he uttered the last digit of the number with his last wheezing gasp. It was a convincing performance. The news crew seemed to buy it, at any rate, and while they stood transfixed, Will came speeding up in the fake ambulance hired for the occasion. He and an office boy from Hazzenack's jumped out dressed in scrubs and surgical masks. They tossed the actor onto a gurney and blasted away with lights flashing.

Will was pretty sure at the time that the news would report the story on its late edition, but he never expected them to *lead* with it. He was surprised they didn't call around to the local hospitals to check on the victim's condition or at least confirm that he'd been admitted. By their next broadcast they would be aware of the mistake, and that would be the end of the story unless some local theatergoer recognized the actor and reported him as risen from the grave and playing Big Daddy in *Cat on a Hot Tin Roof*.

"What's wrong, pal? You okay?"

Will looked at the goateed man, Chaz.

"Yeah, I'm fine. Just thinking about some things."

He glanced around the courtroom. Still no Cissy.

"So what was your wife's decision? What'd she tell you to do?"

"She wanted me to spend more time with her, less time at work. She made me promise to get home on time the next day."

"Ah. Women do demand their attention, don't they? And what'd you tell *her* to do?"

"To get a job."

Chaz chuckled. "Good for you."

Will knew that Cissy had every right to be jealous of his work. He didn't pay her as much attention as he used to, and he'd killed the romantic mood that was developing between them the night his news piece aired. So he agreed when she asked him to clock out at five the following day. *But*, he said, in exchange he wanted her to look for work. He thought she needed to get out and spend more time around people, and searching for a job was the best way he could think of to do that.

Leaving the office on time the next day wasn't a problem. Mr. Hazzenack didn't expect much from him after his heart attack success, so he put in his eight hours and left even though Thurston Grumm was making a fresh pot of coffee in the break room. Grumm's cadaverously thin form stood hunched over the coffeemaker like a buzzard with its head drooping or a snake partly raised from a coiled position. He was upset about the heart attack piece and had been telling people in the office all day that he was working on something big, but he refused to say what the project was. Will figured it would be some variation of the heart attack stunt, because Grumm wasn't very creative. He wasn't very smart, either. Earlier in the day they were both on treadmills when they heard Hazzenack's booming voice on the other side of the big, cubicled office. Will immediately notched his odometer up a mile. Grumm saw him and notched his up too, so Will added another mile, then Grumm did, and they kept going like that back and forth until Hazzenack appeared around a corner. They were both walking furiously fast on their machines by then and Hazzenack smiled when he saw them. He thumped his belly, said, "That's the spirit, boys!" and stopped to look at Will's odometer. It read three miles. He smiled and gave a thumbs-up while Will pretended to be busy on his headphone selling advertising to a boat dealer. Hazzenack didn't interrupt him, just gave him the thumbs-up, and then he stepped over to check Grumm's odometer. Unfortunately for Grumm he hadn't run it back down after the little re-set competition, and it read twenty-two miles. Or that's what Mr. Hazzenack said. "Twenty-two miles?! What the hell are you *doing*, Grumm?!" Grumm didn't help his situation when he held up a silencing finger like he was negotiating a deal on his headphone. "That's right," he said. "We'll get those churches to go Catholic again, Mr. Pope."

So Grumm wasn't very bright, but sometimes he got lucky, and he didn't mind putting in the long hours. Will didn't like leaving him there without knowing more about his secret project, but he took off at five anyway like he promised Cissy he would.

He found her really excited when he got home. "I have a new job!" she squealed as she hugged him.

She'd been hired to set up a bonsai area at Sickley's Greenhouse, where she'd bought maybe a ton of the gardening supplies that filled the back yard and garage. Will was surprised she found work. He merely wanted her to look for a job as a kind of social activity, but he was pleased she actually landed a position. And he was glad she was so happy about it.

They celebrated by going out to eat Mexican food, and then later Cissy's mom, Inga, called. Cissy must have spoken to her during the day and told her about Will's heart attack piece, because Inga never watched TV but wanted to discuss the story with him anyway. She asked if he was happy with himself.

"You know the news media is just a propaganda organ of the government," she said. "And collusion between news and business advertising could be considered fascism. You *do* know that, don't you, Will?"

Will said he wasn't sure what she meant and asked her to elaborate, and she did, in detail it sounded like, judging by the buzzing sound coming from the phone after he put it in his shirt pocket. He was sitting on the back porch and flipping through a magazine for advertising ideas. When the buzzing stopped he spoke into the phone and said he missed some points, and he asked her to repeat her explanation. He didn't listen that time either, or the third and fourth times. Finally he heard her break off in mid buzz and begin barking his name. She'd figured out what he was doing. He returned the phone to Cissy, who was inside working on her dollhouse, and he went back to the peace of the porch to flip through his magazine and contemplate Inga.

She had always been a pain in the ass. She called herself Inga Freer-Farr, an absurdity she came up with after grafting her maiden name onto Eddie Farr's when they got married. Poor Eddie. Inga dominated him like she'd dominated her five kids, including Cissy, and like she wished she could dominate Will. But she couldn't do that, and she disliked him on account of it.

She couldn't help being the way she was, really; she was just an old-time Austin hippie woman, strong-willed and opinionated. Left-wing politics used to take up a lot of her time back when she worked in local cooperatives and skinny dipped in Lake Travis, but then she got married and turned her attention to raising her kids. In between childbirths she worked at landscaping. She built koi ponds and zen gardens and taught feng shui. She'd always been a tall woman and big-boned, but she was now just fat on account of decades of marijuana-induced munchies. Her skin was like elephant hide too, from no telling how many thousands of hours spent in the sun.

Inga browbeat her kids with environmentalism the whole time they were growing up, and as a result they all worked with plants now, even if it was just hobby work with gardens or yards. The browbeating took an odd turn with Cissy. As far as Will could tell she got into the bonsai stuff because of feelings of inadequacy. It was like she knew her work would always be in the shadow of her mom's, so she kept it small.

"What'd you do after that?" Chaz asked. "Was that it, just the one day making each other's decisions?"

Will glanced around and saw that the courtroom was now about half full, but there was still no sign of Cissy.

"No. As a matter of fact, things worked out so well we agreed to do it for two weeks."

Chaz nodded and twisted the tip of his goatee. "I can dig it. So, it's like fate versus self-determination, what you and your wife did. You were free will, taking the initiative and all that, and she was resigned to fate, just accepting what life dished out. But then you reversed things. You forced each other to play the other part."

Will felt a flash of irritation. That's how Cissy described their decision-making swap. She got that kind of thinking from her mom. Sometimes Inga said some pretty mystical things, which could make her sound crazy. Plus she liked to use famous quotes, in an attempt to give her arguments validity, and that made her sound crazy *and* stuck up. And those damned quotes—she had a habit of screwing them up, especially when she was high. You could ask her the time of day, and mixed in with the pot smoke fogging out of her lungs you'd get a mishmash of Jefferson and FDR telling you the only thing we have to fear is time in the course of human events.

Chaz took some receipts from a pocket and thumbed through them, apparently getting ready for his case. Will wondered if Cissy would be bringing any receipts or paperwork, and he thought back to when their decision-making arrangement began to go off the rails. Things were pretty uneventful for the first couple of days, but then he made Cissy mad. He said she should lose some weight. She reacted by saying that Mr. Hazzenack could stand to lose a few pounds too, "with that belly of his. Tell him he needs to spend some time on one of his treadmills." Cissy didn't trust Will to pass the message on, so she made him call her and leave the line on his headphone open while he suggested the exercise regimen to Hazzenack. Of course Hazzenack didn't like the suggestion, and he told Will he needed to do something about his *own* weight. "Start pulling it again. You've been coasting on the heart attack thing long enough."

Will went to the bathroom to stew after the incident, and while he was sitting in a toilet stall he remembered Cissy saying they didn't know what to do with a load of horse manure a truck dumped in the wrong place at her new job. So he called her and told her to volunteer to move it with a shovel and wheelbarrow. He gave her permission to work late if necessary.

Things escalated from there. The two of them began making meaner and meaner decisions for each other, and then Cissy put her mom in charge of Will for the day.

That was on a Sunday. Will had planned to go in to the office for an hour or so to catch up on some paperwork, but Inga wouldn't let him. Instead she made him do fix-up chores around the house. He worked until midnight regrouting tile in the bathroom, and the next day he came up with the money thing that got Cissy arrested.

A middle-aged bailiff in a short-sleeved uniform entered the courtroom at the front, from a corner door that must have led to the judge's chamber. The bailiff was black and his skin had an ashen cast to it. He seemed tired. Will watched him walk slowly down the center aisle, checking people left and right. He paused to answer a couple of questions, and then he reached the double doors at the back of the room. He was about to close them when Inga appeared.

She passed through the doorway with a swaying waddle that made the long folds of her dress/robe thing swirl around her ankles. The material was splotchy purple and yellow and there seemed to be acres of it. Will pictured a hot air balloon deflating and falling on her as she entered the courthouse.

Her long gray hair was pulled back in a ponytail, and an American flag scarf was tied around her head. She told Will she would be wearing the headscarf when he called her on the sly that morning, to turn Cissy's decision-making over to her for the day.

He and Cissy had backed off making decisions for each other since her arrest, but technically there was still one more day to go on their agreement. And Will owed Cissy for letting her mom boss him around for a day, so he called Inga first thing that morning and pretended to be sorry for getting Cissy into a legal jam. He said, "It's my fault she's going to court, and I feel terrible about it." He also said he didn't know what to do for Cissy now that she was looking at jail time, and he wanted her, Inga, to help.

It wasn't like him to be open with her, so it didn't surprise him when he heard the click of a lighter over the phone. She was wary and firing up a joint to aid in her cogitations. She lit the joint, vacuumed in, held, then on the exhale she asked how she could help.

"Well, I'd like for you to make Cissy's decisions today, the way you made mine for me last week. That would mean appearing in court, and I hate to put that on you, but with your lofty ideals and speaking ability . . ." He tossed in a fake sniffle. "Well, with you presenting her case, she might be able to avoid a stint on the chain gang."

To his delight, Inga rose to the bait like the whale she was. They went over the particulars of the case as she made blowhole sounds working her joint, and by the time Will heard her stub it out she was telling him about the flag scarf she planned to wear, to show she was patriotic.

"Yeah," he encouraged, "that's a good idea," and then he remembered her peace symbol earrings. "And what about your big loop earrings? The gold ones? Wear those, too. That'll show you're peaceful."

"Well . . . I don't know. Some of those judges are pretty fascistic, but I guess I could wear them. They're clip-ons, so if he looks belligerent I can just slip them off."

And she'd dressed like she said she would, with the flag scarf on her head and the peace symbol earrings brushing her fat-humped shoulders. She looked like an enormous, patriotic, pacifist pirate as she came in through the courtroom's doors. Or an air pirate fallen out of the sky and struggling to free herself from the folds of her collapsed balloon. She waddled up the center aisle with a sideways buttcrack of a smile serenely creasing her leathery face. Will knew that somehow she'd managed to burn a quick joint before entering the halls of justice.

Cissy was a step behind her. She'd been hidden by Inga's immensity when they passed through the doorway, but Will saw her once they were inside. She was wearing her dark gray dress with the calf-length skirt and long sleeves. Very proper, very conservative. Unlike Inga, Cissy didn't look serene—she looked unsure and nervous.

Inga saw Will and started toward him, but Cissy reached forward and hooked a hand under one of her arms. She steered her to a bench on the other side of the aisle. They sat side by side, three rows back from Will.

Cissy glared at him, no doubt still angry from finding out at the last minute that she would need to drive to South Austin to pick up her mom. Will hadn't told her that he and Inga spoke, and he was sipping a leisurely second cup of coffee when Cissy received her pickup call. She dashed out of the house after grabbing a handful of makeup so she could finish getting ready in the car.

The bailiff closed the doors, walked to the front of the room and stood in front of the judge's bench.

"All rise for the honorable Judge Anthony Moorehead."

Everyone stood as the judge came in from the door at the front corner of the room. When he was in his chair the bailiff said they could sit again, then he moved to a side wall, sighed tiredly and stood with his hands clasped behind his back.

The judge was an older guy with liver spots visible through his thin gray hair. He wore a black robe but Will could see a red bow tie not completely covered at the throat. The man had a jolly, relaxed face, and he smiled down at the paperwork in front of him as he shuffled through it. A minute or so passed, then he looked up and smiled at the people in the courtroom. He delivered a speech he must have made hundreds, maybe thousands of times before.

He said that his was just a small claims court, so it was the no-frills version of what they were accustomed to seeing on TV. There was no witness box, because people just stood up and gave their testimony from where they were. Also, there were no tables for attorneys, because attorneys weren't required for such minor litigation.

The first case he called involved a psychiatrist and one of his patients. A woman. She refused to pay for an office visit. It had been her first session and she said it was a mistake. The psychiatrist filed a motion to make her pay.

The judge said he was surprised the case was in a small claims court, since psychiatrists normally charged such exorbitant rates.

"My rates aren't that high," the shrink said. He was in his fifties, with salt and pepper hair, and dressed in an expensive pinstriped suit. "I do volume business because I undercut the competition."

"And you get what you pay for," the patient said. She was a dowdy middle-aged woman squeezed into a shiny blue dress that showed her bra strap in back.

"Please elaborate," the judge said.

"Sure. I told the doctor I was concerned for myself because they say that possessing great beauty can drive a woman insane."

"And how did he respond to that?" the judge asked.

"He said I seemed a little neurotic."

Will heard some muffled laughter behind him, and someone whispered, "Well, she ain't no looker."

The judge gaveled the court into silence and issued his ruling.

"It's true that you get what you pay for, but in this case the defendant won't have to pay. The doctor may write the session off as a business loss if he wants, and he has ten days to produce his license to practice psychiatry to the court."

Next the judge called a case involving a man named Charles Guzman. He meant Chaz, the goateed man sitting next to Will.

It turned out that Chaz ran a porno shop, and he was there because a customer wanted a refund on a video he'd bought. The customer was a pudgy guy, pale, in his late twenties. He wore a necktie tucked beneath the collar of a stretched-out T-shirt, and when the judge asked him to present his case he held up a DVD and said he got ripped off. He said the actors in the video talked too much, mostly tallying up the cost for a prostitute's services. The video was called *The Sum of Her Holes.* The judge chuckled and said he should rightfully recess to view the evidence, but he wouldn't, and then he let Chaz tell his side of the story. Chaz claimed the customer was just crabby. He said he knew the type, and he offered to swap the video for another. "One for premature ejaculators. It's called *Cum in the Door.*"

The judge ruled for a flat refund and then joked again that he should view the evidence.

Chaz squeezed past Will on his way out. He met up with the disgruntled customer in the center aisle and used a couple of hand lotion coupons to gruntle him again on the way to the exit.

Cissy's case was next. "Cloyndarter's Miniatures versus Mrs. Cecelia Deeds," the judge announced. He read over some paperwork, to himself, then he said, "Mr. Cloyndarter has detailed his case against Mrs. Deeds in his statement, so I'll start by hearing from Mrs. Deeds."

Cissy stood. She was still nervous and Will felt sorry for her as she tried to explain her side of the story to the judge. Instead of telling about the incident in Cloyndarter's shop, she rambled on about the decision-making switch and the trouble it had caused.

The judge stopped her.

"I understand, Mrs. Deeds. You and your husband are having problems at home, but we're not here to discuss this decision-making issue. We're here to consider how you affected the business of Mr. Cloyndarter. He says in his statement that you refused to pay him for some merchandise." He looked around the courtroom. "Is Mr. Cloyndarter here?"

"I'm here, your honor."

Cloyndarter stood up. He was a slender young man, with short-trimmed blonde hair, and dressed in a white linen suit and red shirt. He stood resting his hands on a black walking stick.

"And your business is 'Cloyndarter's Miniatures'?" the judge asked.

"Yes, sir."

"In your statement you say that Mrs. Deeds refused to pay for some pots she broke. Petit pots, you call them. I take it those are miniature flowerpots."

"That's correct, your honor. They're *exquisite* little pots, from Paraguay, handcrafted by Guillermo. Each one is as thin as a chocolate shaving on top of cappuccino whipped cream."

The judge seemed at a loss for words for a moment, then he cleared his throat and said, "Yes, well, uh . . ." He looked at Cissy. "Did you handle those pots in Mr. Cloyndarter's shop, Mrs. Deeds?"

"Yes, sir. I was thinking of using them to do a bonsai flower project, to keep the root balls small."

"And you accidentally broke some when you were handling them?"

"Yes, sir."

"Then why didn't you pay for them?"

"I tried to, but Mr. Cloyndarter wouldn't cooperate."

"In his statement he says he *did* cooperate. He offered to let you pay in various ways, even with a personal check, which he doesn't normally accept."

"I know, your honor, but the check didn't clear. I tried that after my credit card was declined. My husband froze our accounts so I couldn't use them."

Cissy scowled at Will, and he recalled how the money freeze was just a passing thought he'd had the morning after Inga made him do the job on the bathroom tile. He was still pretty upset as he sat in his cubicle at work and cleaned grout from under his fingernails, and he remembered that Cissy said she would be going shopping later. So he decided to aggravate her by messing with her money. He made the phone calls ordering the freezes when he finished with his nails, but he never thought the calls would lead to her getting arrested.

During his lunch break he went to pay Cissy's bail. He wanted to stretch the process out, so when he got to the jail he said he didn't recognize her from her mugshot. He asked to see her in person, in one of those viewing rooms with the see-through mirror.

The cops assisting him grumbled but arranged the viewing, and Will watched as they led Cissy into a barren gray room and made her back up against a wall with height stripes on it. She glared at the mirror as he asked them to make her turn to the left, then to the right, and then to tap dance in circles. The cops were glaring at him by then too, so he finally paid her bail and signed her out.

The judge said, "Well if you couldn't pay with a credit card or check, Mrs. Deeds, why didn't you use cash?"

"Because I didn't have enough on me. And I couldn't go home to get any because he told me I had to pay before I left the shop."

"That's because she broke so *many* of the pots," Cloyndarter said. "I *had* to demand payment, but she didn't have it, so I called the gendarmes."

"Do you have the money with you now?" the judge asked Cissy.

"Yes, sir."

"And are you willing to reimburse?"

"Yes, sir. I'd be glad to—"

"Excuse me," Inga interrupted. She struggled to her feet with a lot of arm flapping and grunting. "Whew. My son-in-law has asked me to make decisions for Cissy, your honor. I mean, for Mrs. Deeds."

The judge rubbed a temple and said, "The decision-making again. I guess someone better explain that part of things to me after all. But first, exactly who are you, ma'am?"

"Inga Freer-Farr, the defendant's mother."

Lifting her bulk off the bench created a ripple in the still air of the courtroom, kind of like a new island rising in the ocean, Will thought. Inga's scent washed up to him as she shifted on her feet and settled into a more comfortable standing position. Will whiffed the patchouli oil she wore to mask marijuana smoke, then he picked up undercurrents of honeysuckle and lime. Inga liked her herbal soaps and shampoos.

The judge said, "Thank you, Mrs. Freer-Farr, but as I explained earlier, people represent themselves in this court."

"Which is what I'm doing. My daughter surrendered her decision-making to her husband, and he turned it over to me, so in point of fact I'm representing herself."

The judge rubbed his temple again and looked at Cissy.

"Is this the way you want it, Mrs. Deeds?"

"It's . . . what we all agreed to, your honor."

"Okay. Then I guess I'll allow it." The judge looked at Inga, who was standing with her chin thrust out. "And I've been a judge long enough to know when someone is primed to go rhetorical, Mrs. Freer-Farr, so go ahead. Have your say."

"I shall, your honor. But allow me to center myself first."

Will watched as Cissy sat down and Inga closed her eyes to gather her thoughts. Everyone in the courtroom was focused on her flag-capped purple and yellow bulk. Will wondered if she'd be quoting from Gandhi or Che Guevara.

After a moment Inga opened her eyes and laid one hand on the back of the bench in front of her. She placed the other hand over her heart and fixed a serious gaze on the judge.

"We are now engaged in a great contest," she intoned. "Each of the parties in this marriage have surrendered their free will, to test whether they can long endure." She was going with Lincoln. Sort of. "It's the age-old battle of trying to figure out whether we control our own destinies or are slaves to the whims of fate. Are we action or reaction? These two are trying to figure out what makes us human. Are we conceived in liberty or dedicated to the proposition of unemancipated karma? That's the crux of the issue under consideration here, the yin and the yang of it, and I for one hope they bring forth upon this continent an answer. I also hope that their findings, like your honor's finding in favor of my daughter, shall not perish from this earth."

Inga seemed to have the whole courtroom baffled, or drugged by some narcotic mixture of her exotic scents, and when she finished speaking she crossed her arms over her huge bosom and thrust her chin out even farther. Her Abraham Lincoln pose, Will guessed, though it would have been more effective if she'd been wearing a stovepipe hat instead of a red, white and blue headscarf.

The judge said, "Well, fate wins this round. The defendant will pay for the broken pots, plus fifty dollars for inconveniencing Mr. Cloyndarter." He rapped his gavel, chuckled and spoke to himself. "'Shall not perish.' I need to put a court reporter in my next budget request."

* * *

Three weeks later Will was sprawled on the couch and watching a video of Thurston Grumm. It was probably the hundredth time he'd seen it, and it always made him smile.

The video was of a publicity stunt Grumm pulled—the idea he'd been keeping a secret at the office. But like Will thought he might, Grumm merely did a variation of the candy store heart attack.

He stalked a local news crew that was on assignment, and when they came out of a coffee shop he staged a fake suicide. He didn't hire an actor because, as he explained to Mr. Hazzenack later, he wanted to cut costs by putting on a disguise and playing the part himself. So he held a pistol to his afro-wigged head, and once the camera was on him he said he intended to shoot himself on the count of three.

Things didn't go the way he planned, though. As soon as he declared his intention to self-destruct, a police car happened to pull up in front of the coffee shop. The toy store Grumm was trying to plug ended up getting a lot more exposure than it wanted.

Grumm's plan was to put the gun to his head and count to three, and between one and two say, "I wish I'd treated my children better," then between two and three say, "I should have taken them shopping at Naudell's Toys more often." And then on three he would pull the trigger. Of course the gun would click on an empty chamber, and while everyone cringed and screamed he would scamper off. But then the cops drove up and he saw that he wouldn't be able to scamper, so he didn't pull the trigger on three. He kept counting, and he ad-libbed about the toy store while he did. He gave their address and phone number, and named some of the employees, and on the count of ten the reporter asked him exactly how the toy store had driven him to suicide. On the count of twelve the cops threatened to shoot him themselves if he didn't stop blocking the entrance to the coffee shop. He was left with no alternative but to surrender.

The toy store filed a lawsuit against Hazzenack's Adverdazzling and Mr. Hazzenack fired Grumm. The bad PR caused business to fall off, and Will and the other employees were told to avoid overtime until things picked up again.

So Will and Cissy's experiment with decision-making had worked out, more or less. They each got what they wanted—Cissy was able to spend more time with Will because he was working normal hours, and Will was happy because Cissy was occupied during the day with her greenhouse job.

The police finished handcuffing Grumm on the video. Will used the remote to run it back to the beginning, and as it got off to its slow start he looked at Cissy.

She was sitting cross-legged on the floor, at the end of the coffee table, leaning over a tray of little bonsai flowers in their petit pots. She had on the pink shorts he liked so much. He thought she looked sexy in a geeky sort of way, with the jeweler's glasses pulled down on her head and the tip of her tongue pinched between her lips in concentration.

Thankfully she was over being mad at him, and he was wondering if he could finagle her into bed for a little fun and games, when she looked at him. Her green eyes were big and shimmery from the magnifier. "Can we go see mom?" she asked.

Will forgot about sex. The visits to Inga were *far* better than sex.

Following her Gettysburg Address about fate in the courtroom, Inga had raised her fist to the judge and announced her Declaration of Independence from his fascism. It shocked Will how quickly the old guy went from jolly to hopping mad. He sentenced Inga to thirty days for contempt, and the bailiff shook off his fatigue and hustled her away.

Will thought of Inga in her orange jumpsuit as Grumm said, "I'm going to shoot myself" on TV. Cissy stood up and stretched her shapely little legs.

Will smiled. Life couldn't get much better.

William Doreski

The Big Departure

More porous than a bath sponge
I'm seeking medical aid
wherever I can find it.

The local hospital has collapsed
in a heap of yellow brick, crushing
the nurses with long painted nails

and the doctors who bought Porsches
to overcome midlife crises.
So I've come to the city where screams

linger in the jagged night air
and the howl of an ambulance
draws almost no one's attention.

The famous hospital where three
Presidents have died of old age
sports a glossy new wing. I enter

with my insurance card held
before me like Achilles' shield.
The click of keyboards replaces

the scratch of pen on paper
that rattled Kafka's heroes
and triggered intolerable angst.

I describe my symptoms: the light
pouring through my organs, rain
inflating me like a pumpkin.

The triage nurse declares I've no pulse
so I can wait my turn in a crowd
of fellow water-solubles.

This is it: the big departure,
the silence looming at my back.
Eventually a brown-shoe doctor

examines my skin and declares it
an authentic bit of parchment
from the Byzantine era when men

were women and women were shrines
around which displaced gods sulked.
Dismissed with a prescription

I re-enter the city with tears
furrowed in my face and a limp
that will earn me space in a hostel

where homeless men pass through
each other not like ghosts but
indifferent as quantum debris.

Jailed Again

A gnarly brown wool blanket
and a food bowl shaped like a dog's.
Cellmates cuddle against me

to catch my intellectual warmth.
The day elongates. Nothing to do
but sleep in earth tones impervious

to onslaughts of nerve. Lawyers
eager to obfuscate their clients
peer through the bars, their faces

lit by flint on steel. Bondsmen
sneer through snags of facial hair
and flap their old-fashioned wallets.

I think I'm undercover,
but can't be sure a vicious crime
hasn't happened far away,

framing me in the sepia
of an old family photograph.
At last I roll out of my bunk

without disturbing three inmates
snoring in three languages.
A guard whispers that I'm free—

and now I'm standing knee-deep
in a marsh gone brown with autumn.
Was I actually imprisoned?

Did I complete my assignment,
overhear and report a plot
to foil the Republican Party?

I believe I failed. The mud exerts
powerful suction and drags me
backward as I clomp toward shore.

Two steps forward, one back.
I flop in dry oak leaves the color
of the blanket in my cell

If I hadn't roiled the marsh water,
exciting its parasites, I'd cup
a handful and drink. I'm free,

aren't I? The hard light shudders
and a cloud shaped like a zeppelin
obscures, for a moment, the sigh

I've released against my will,
and a halfhearted thunderclap
attempts to pretend to applaud.

Criminal, Victim, or Witness

Clues include tire tracks gouged
into bedrock, cigar butts
smoldering, and the wrapper
of a fatal chocolate bar.
You haven't reported a crime,

but I'm following large and hairy
tracks through drifting snow, sniffing
the air for blood spoor. Yesterday
on a subway train a woman
twenty years older than me

offered her seat. As the cars rattled
over the Longfellow Bridge
the Boston skyline gnashed and ground
like ill-fitting dentures. Today
with the great storm upon us

I'm unsure whether I'm tracing
criminal, victim, or witness.
Since you and I have occupied
those roles, often more than one
at once, I suspect that woman

has followed me to New Hampshire
and smoked a few tough cigars
and driven hard over ledge
to unwrap that deadly confection
and tease my childish appetites.

I know you've seen her peering
into my study with infinite
longing. Yesterday the gloom
lay over Boston like a sheet
of fiberglass insulation. Now

in the dense and lovely storm-light
that woman's hiding in the woods,
conspiring with the weather and you
to erase me from myself forever,
leaving barely a trace of ghost.

Moon

Man playing guitar
wishes it were a cigar box,
the Mississippi a snake—

one he could wear around his neck
and train to sing the chorus
to impress the girl serving drinks.

Lighting a fire between his hands,
he starts another song
making all the bottles in the room
heavy over the neon.
Flung,

they break into few pieces,
get picked up
and dropped into a pay phone.

Under somebody else's moon,
the barrelhouse—as any burning
barn—falls
quiet when lightning dries.

Man signs a beer coaster,
stops to call his daughter
but only hears the sound of a train.
The waitress counting tips
picks glass out of her curls,

listens to him hum
about two devils and honey—
one named Daddy,
one named Shine.

A Collection

John Stack IV

Confessions of a Southern Gentleman

A Ghost Story

"Tell me a story," she whispered, as her arms tightened on my torso. "One of yours."

So in a low-key, cool cadence . . .

* * *

It was just past midnight when I finally got home—damn tempest. I was soaking wet and only wanting a drink when I entered the darkness. I reached for the bottle—the day was over and now it was time for it to die a proper death. I began to pour the whiskey, then froze—

"What's that smell? Impossible."

I quit pouring and downed the glass.

I turned among the shadows and began to cross the room—that smell. A decoction of orchids, vines, jasmine, and who knows what else she found on a trip to Haiti. I love it, and haven't smelled it for seven years.

No one except her wears it.

"But she's gone, in the ground for seven years now," I said to myself. "Seven long and lonely years."

I reached my hand for the bedroom door. It was closed—I never close it. Not anymore.

I took a deep breath—the smell was stronger.

If I opened that door to an empty room—as it should be—then what people had said for years was true.

I was crazy.

Who walks into the darkness thinking of a dead love and expects to find her on the other side of a closed door—seven years later? A crazy man, that's who.

I took a deep breath, turned the knob, and let out a long sigh of relief—at least I wasn't crazy.

* * *

I trailed off reading and looked at her.

She was asleep. So peaceful. So beautiful.

I took a deep breath—I could smell her skin: orchids, vines, and jasmine.

Rabbit Holes

"I AM FREAKING OUT!" she yelled in vivid panic. I couldn't help but be slightly amused; nevertheless, "What's the problem, love?" I ask in the most soothing timbre I can compose.

"I'm conscious, and I know I'm conscious so I know I have a mind," she began on the border of despair; otherwise, I'd have asked her where her mind is located, exactly. But I behaved, and let her continue, grinning all the while. "But you, or the rest of the world for that matter . . . how can I know that you have one too? or that they're similar at all? or that you, or all of this," she waved her hands through the air, "is not just some delusion, that it's not just in my head?!"

"But it is," I said under my breath, immediately drawing her eyes from the sky to me. There is no possible way to describe in the human language the look on her face.

"What?" she whispered timidly.

"What what? Is there a problem?" I asked with equanimity, which precipitated her mien of alarm into one of gravitas as she injuncted, "Don't fuck with me."

"I wouldn't dream of it," I assured her.

She didn't buy it. Her eyes grew narrow with suspicion. "Really? Then promise—"

I cut her off. "However, if I had, I would've asked you since you think that all of this might be in your head, then God might be too, right?"

Her eyes instantly dilated in full. "Don't even start—"

I cut her off again. "Because if you were thinking that, then I was going to set your mind and soul at ease."

"How?"

"By telling you that cannot be. If you think that all of this is in your mind, and that God is just in your mind, then that means that you can imagine something more powerful outside of your mind, something not just limited to it."

She was totally rapt; I continued.

"And since you can imagine something more powerful, that means consequently there must be something more powerful, since nothing can be more powerful than God at the point where the limits of your mind and imagination or mine or anyone's for that matter end. He is there doing what He does, right?"

"Yes," she agreed diffidently, but started to calm down.

"And that means that me," I patted my chest, and then I pointed to the sky and waved, "all of this, is not just in your mind, right?"

She sighed in relief. "Yeah, makes senses. Thanks for talking me back from the edge of insanity." She leaned forward and gave me a quick kiss, then leaned back just as quickly.

"You're quite welcome," I reassured her, then reached to the plastic bowl beside me, pulling out two sugar cubes. I placed one in my mouth and extended the other to her.

"I don't know . . ." She hesitated, she pondered, she capitulated, taking it from my hand.

"I thought that while we just established you might not can count on your thoughts, you can count on mine." I smiled.

She smiled. "You know these roads well?" She placed the cube on her tongue and let it melt.

And down the rabbit hole she came to find me.

Not Yet

Tell me you love me;
But no, not yet.
First perform with me
All the acts that love forbids,
For fear of injury;
Then afterwards,
Lying in a pool of our sweat
Tell me you love me;
But no, not yet.

On Being

"Do you see that tree over there?" I asked you. "Is it being or becoming?"

"Being," you told me, and then quickly changed your mind. "Becoming," you said, "for it's not yet reduced to its final form."

"Its potential, you meant to say?" I offered; you nodded. "And what if someone was to come, cut the tree down, take it away and make a chair or a bookcase of it?"

"It would be in its final form then," you readily replied. "Save were it to be destroyed and returned to the earth, feeding the earth, and starting the whole process over again."

"Fair enough. Then let me ask you this: Can you ever look at something made from wood and not know that it's made of wood, or that it came from a larger piece; or that someone, similar to us, fashioned it to please someone like us?"

"Of course not. Besides, that last part is just plain foolishness: everything is created to please someone or something, the original efficacy. Eye of the beholder, you know?"

"And what were we made for?" I prompted you. Your immediate response doesn't fail to impress. "Each other, obviously."

"And where did we come from?"

"You mean biologically? From our parents . . . but that's not what you meant, is it?"

I shook my head. "Did it ever strike you odd that your memories, like mine, like everyone's, subjective as they are, we recall so many of them from a third-person point of view, seeing them as onlookers and not as ourselves?"

"I'd never thought about it quite like that."

"Things made of wood, come from trees. Things made of metal, come from the various metal ores. There is no doubt that someone similar to ourselves created each object that we behold with someone in mind."

"Your point being?"

"Us." I point to you and then to me. "Not our bodies, for they are but vehicles, but our minds, our souls, they come from somewhere . . . we came from somewhere before we arrived here." I extended my arm. "Something larger than just this," indicating the flesh. "Some call it God, others a universal soul, and others Brahman . . ."

"Then why don't we remember any of that?"

"Think about it. At one moment, a moment which has lasted forever, has no beginning or end so we think, or would think if it mattered, but we're in a state beyond such mundane thoughts. A state of bliss. Then, all of the sudden, we're separated from that, which would be shocking enough in itself, and then the next thing we know, or rather, the first, we're confined—a state we did not know or could even comprehend before. We don't know what to do or how to do it. This is terra incognita in the true sense. We don't realize where we are or what is going on, what this strange body is we are now inhabiting, we don't even know what a body is or the depths to which we have been circumscribed. That experience by itself, let alone becoming acclimated to this new reality and how to function in the vehicle which we have incarnated without instructions, would cause a shock so thorough that it would efface any traces of memories, or what are akin to memories in an ethereal state. We'd be so overwhelmed the only thing we could do is—"

"Scream. Cry. Post-traumatic stress in the strictest sense."

"No doubt."

"Hmm."

"But then as the years progress, and we calm down from the initial scare, we can begin to look past ourselves into our surroundings. There are clues once we piece them together that can't show us everything we feel like we should know. We're still bound to this world, after all; but they do show us vestiges of something much larger. Those traces impress upon our souls adumbrations of something much larger still, and a sort of resignation sets in that we cannot know now, not directly, the answers to the questions that we are looking for. But that's all right. We at least recognize that they are there."

"All in due time."

"Right," I affirmed. "All we can do now is enjoy the ride and make the best of it, for we're certainly committed to it."

"That's all this is, one big ride?"

"Maybe so."

"And what does it mean to ride?" you asked, all bright-eyed.

I just shook my head and listened.

"To ride, in essence, means to move. Either way, riding is a verb; and a verb is motion," said you.

Smart soul.

"And what is motion?"

"Deus est motus," said I.

And here we are again.

ubiety

She was sitting in the lush grass, a sea of deep green peppered all over with perhaps a thousand different kinds of flowers; yet her eyes were all but vacant as she gazed with a melancholy air to the ocean of blue above. Curiosity got the better of me so I walked over and sat beside her. We sat in silence for several minutes before I finally broke the spell.

"Penny for your thoughts."

"Doldrums are a hell of a thing. Glad they're ephemeral."

"Glad that you remember that they are." I clasped my hand around hers.

"Unfortunately, that's no real consolation at the moment." She grinned.

"Too true. There's no rationalizing with emotions; they've a will of their own."

She sighed in resignation, but, at the same time . . . afflatus!

"A wise man once said that there is no arguing with a mood; it can be changed by some fortunate event, or by a change in our bodily condition, but it cannot be changed by argument." I then positioned myself behind her and began to massage her shoulders, her neck, her back. She said nothing, neither for nor against, but I could feel her muscles loosening; and, what's more, I could feel her breathing change as it took to a slower, contented rhythm. I continued this for the better part of ten minutes and not a word was passed until, "Lie on your stomach," I suggested. I rubbed. She did not hesitate. As she maneuvered, I stopped her. "Let's take this off." I reached for the bottom of her small sundress. She raised her arms as I slid the amber and gold over her shoulders. Her little white cotton panties and bra were in perfect relief upon her body—tanned, toned, and curved in just the right spots.

I was speechless—hypnotized, mesmerized, paralyzed—all of the above.

She slowly turned her head, sweeping a dark strand of hair behind her ear as she did. Her eyes met mine, her sapphires coruscating in the sun shone on me and me alone. At the corners of her lips and eyes small curves began to form, the slightest of smiles.

I continued to look on.

There are moments in our lives which we can recall so lucidly and with such ease that they are forever part of who we are. A glimpse of divinity stays with us all of our days, always reminding us of both the paradise on earth we are fortunate enough to experience, and the paradise to come once we leave this world behind. It is a forerunner of that which is to come.

The presence of angels is the herald of paradise, and there was an angel before me to be certain.

Rêve

It was the old farmhouse I was returning to
with Aunt Ida, who wanted
to see my mother and father,
long dead,
to a house remembered as it was
half a century ago.

Unpainted pickets
ash-weathered, hollyhocks
pink and ragged,
the old barn
oxblood red and crammed with junk
(old Victrolas, army trunks,
rusted garden tools)
hayloft floor rotted
on verge of collapsing.

The major difference, the yard itself,
grass and weeds now mud and stones.
The car we're in stalls out before we see
tangling concord vines,
wisteria in the pear tree,
the house once again brick red
too distant for reality.

Everywhere we look are cats,
curled and sleeping,
lounging or alert,
watchful with feet tucked under them,

as we climb the slick uncertain
treacherous
path to the back door
to confront
in all its muddy slippage,
our human past.

Lobo

The wolf who lives with me
stays second in the pack
because I growl at him at midnight
moving him out of
the best part of the bed.

The wolf who lives with me
wails with distant ambulances, singing
as if he's found his former tribe.

The wolf who lives with me
herds postal carriers, cats
and tries to herd me
until I growl at him again.

The wolf who lives with me
paces from fence to fence,
antic, anticipating enemies (or squirrels)
who breach the sidewalk or the porch.

The wolf who lives with me
second-in-command,
as guardian of this triple-specied pack
makes sure that all his beings
return to their proper caves
each nightfall.

Tom Conlan

Opening Day

The evening before the trout opener, Doc and I scouted a small stream flowing under the blacktop a couple bends down from the farm. Almost seventy-two, Doc feels weak sometimes and likes to fish closer to home.

Snow stayed late this spring, giving hope the water levels would be up and trout could find a place to hide under overhanging stream banks. Doc parked his truck by the large culvert where the creek passes below the road. We walked the old railroad grade past pockets of blackened snow and ice lying on the north side of small crevices hidden from the sun. The sound of baying hound dogs followed us down the raised, rocky path. Though careful not to slam the doors climbing out of the truck, we had spooked the dogs, hidden somewhere in a kennel nearby.

A half mile down the grade, a bridge crosses Orr Creek. The current funneling under the bridge forms a wide pool on the downstream side. Cedar logs long fallen across the stream in natural chaotic patterns provide structure for brook trout.

Doc and I looked down from ten feet above happy to see the water level healthy and the creek flowing strong. Doc pointed. "Look at that shit-tangle. We'll have to fish with light rods from the bank."

We hiked around the low-lying swamp upstream of the bridge and hunted for spots where a guy could cast without losing a hook. Without our hip boots, we stayed on higher ground and had to cross over a few old rusted fences bent down or broken by years of fishermen refusing to acknowledge the creek as private property. Satisfied after finding a few promising ledges cut out by the meandering stream, we hiked back down the grade. A backdrop of never-tiring howling hounds grew louder as we approached the road. "Did you see the 'posted' sign?" Doc asked.

"No," I said. I had not seen the sign and I forgot to look on the way out.

Doc dropped me off at the farm. As he backed out, he rolled down the window and said, "I don't want to get up at the crack of dawn. I'll call you when I wake up or you call me."

* * *

I usually rise with the sun but on this day, rolled over several times for some much needed sleep. Between turns and short but effective restful periods, I looked out the window to a glorious sunny morning, and traveled back to the Saturdays of my youth waking to a new, clear day and nothing to do but enjoy the world. Startled from a dream by the ringing phone next to the bed, I answered "Hello" in a sleepy, low, gruff voice.

Doc, not a master of cell phones, thought he reached a wrong number, responded questioning, "Hello, Tom?"

After two useless rounds of the conversation, Doc said, "Are you still in fuckin' bed? I'm on my way out from town. Get moving."

The face of my old clock radio read nine a.m. The sun had been up since six. I put on the coffee, let Stella our German shepherd out to run, and lay down on the rug in my study to stretch. Five minutes into stretching Doc walked in the front door calling, "Tom?"

Glenda, hardly awakened by the commotion, yelled from bed, "He's in his study."

Doc walked through the living room and, seeing me on the floor in flannel shorts and a tee shirt, said, "I'm going out on the porch for a smoke. Call me when the coffee's ready."

* * *

Sometime after ten, Doc parked a hundred yards up the road from the creek crossing. We had put on our hip boots before leaving the farm and quietly began the walk up the grade. Spring peepers sang a symphony from the low-lying swampy forest surrounding the old railroad bed. We heard turkeys gobbling, and then saw a mature tom with a long-hanging wattle hiding in the woods. Halfway to the bridge, the hounds joined the band.

About forty feet before reaching the bridge, Doc said, "Let's get our rods ready here."

We tiptoed slowly to the edge of the concrete covering the bridge culvert. Doc smiled. "Go ahead, take the first cast."

I laid a panther martin perfectly into the current and let it float down to a small pool formed by a downed cedar tree and slowly reeled back the swimming spinner. Nothing. Doc cast, also with no luck. Both of us knew the likelihood of a brook trout hitting diminished directly with the number of casts into a pool. We alternated for a few minutes. "I might have had a bite," he called, our spirits rising.

Wanting to test the new knee I had installed ten weeks earlier, I climbed down the bank, leaving the broad pool for Doc to fish from above. I worked my way downstream fishing little runs where the creek narrowed, and spots where the current undercut the bank. Somewhere in my head I knew the stream was too cold, that we were too early in the year and too early in the day. The sun needed to warm the water and wake the trout. But I still pushed downstream, careful not to stumble on exposed roots, my face slapped by wayward bushes along the bank. I waded across and found a large bend. "A trout must live here," I thought, but an empty cast disappointed again.

On the other bank, I found a clearer path to walk back to the bridge. Doc was gone, I figured a half mile upstream around the swamp where we walked the previous evening. I climbed down the bank on the upstream side. I could fish my way along the creek and likely run into him.

Continually caught by pine branches and bushes in the snarly swamp, I looked for a place to enter the water and wade. I spotted a green grass ledge and while slowly pulling a fresh, reddish purple tag alder strand out of the way, paused, noticing the first fuzzy grey bud of spring just inches from my eyes. I stepped in the water. The cool spring run sucked the legs of my hip boots against my jeans like a soothing compress. I looked up and noticed a small creek, about eight feet wide, entering the main stream just ahead. I realized that this was Skinner Creek, which drained the land for several miles to the northwest, including the swampy trickle flowing through my farm. I had named the trickle Black Creek after the black mud my old yellow lab, Chet, would bring home, his legs covered following a romp in the rich dark muck.

I worked slowly upstream following Skinner Creek, planning each step through tight trees. Whenever I looked down for a place to step, I caught the hook of the Panther Martin on a branch above and took some time to set it free. I came to an island outcrop in the center of the creek dividing the water into two flows. One side turned and cascaded like a miniature waterfall. The far side flowed in a straight run, and the two met again ten feet below, where a cedar tree shaded the rejoined stream.

I took a deep breath, certain that this bend would hold a brook trout. I dropped the lure into the water, and let out a few feet of line to tempt any fish living by the bank near the cedar. I saw a silver flash and felt a tug, then a release. I reeled in and dropped again, several times, and each time he tugged and then let go. I saw he was a small trout, not a legal keeper, but at least I had felt a tug on this opening day.

I hiked back out of the creek bottom, saw Doc sitting on the ground by the bridge, and plopped down next to him. I bummed a smoke and we swapped stories. I told him about my one bite. He said, "I thought you'd wade to the log bridge upstream."

Turning to his creel, Doc pulled out two speckled, fifteen-inch brook trout and said, "I got them both below the log bridge."

Astonished, happy for Doc but frustrated, I could only reply, "Fuck me."

We talked a while before Doc reached back in the creel and lifted out the two trout. The fish seemed a little dull in color, then he turned one, and I saw that it had been cleaned.

Smiling slyly, Doc said, "I took them out of my freezer this morning."

Laughing like kids on a Saturday morning, we walked back down the railroad grade to the waiting truck. We stopped several times to listen to the turkeys gobbling and tried to spot them in the woods. On the way out, I turned and saw the yellow "Posted—No Trespassing" sign attached to a worn tree stump. The hounds howled while we sat on the tailgate and pulled off our hip boots.

Harvey Schwartz

Twilight Time

Sunset wails its sax
as jazzed up tulips
color the Sound.

Skagit's muddy autumn mess
now levitates in pastels,
like a Persian carpet ride.

Such as mine, on a ferry to Orcas
where I bathe in light.

Thick colored fog
backdrops the sun's
daily fall from grace.

I search for stillness
as color explodes
then disappears,
erases thought.

This pebbled beach on Orcas,
little more than rocks and stones,
has taught me much, I know.

Mt. Baker's plain white dress
shimmers, its new Jovani evening gown
screams to leapfrog my frozen concepts.

North Beach does a
back flip while
black stone's
wavy striations,
whisper, *take me*. I do.

Waves crash with foam
a floating heron, two
seagulls settling on rocks.

My mind thuds to a stop,
while moonrise cello
joins gulls cacophony
and plays colors of wheat,
onto Sucia trees.

A small plane
tips wings hello,
pilot adrift in
shared bathtub of pink.

The sunset drifts away
and lays down its sax.

Moon, cello
and me.
alone

I make my decision.

The End

Crystal sky shatters
to broken glass.

Cutting crop of
once fertile fields
covered in ash.

Black stripes
on trains
breathe smoke,
ghosts stacked

like firewood
as spectacles fall
at train's recoil,
journey's end.

Satan drums to
Munch's scream
snarling, fangs
Cerberus calls,

sky impales
goose-steps
of bloody feet that
shadow the train.

Whispers of
time's muted cries
are lost to me

as spinning wheels
screech, to a stop.

Nonfiction

Rosemary Gregory

The Pink Coat

1949

I believe in pink. I believe happy girls are the prettiest girls. I believe that
tomorrow is another day, and ... I believe in miracles.
—Audrey Hepburn

Sometimes I feel things before I know them. One of those times, the first I remember, was in 1949. I was three at the time and Seattle was emerging from a long war and a wet, gray winter. The suggestions of renewal that I felt were all around me, marinating my young life in a soup of hope and optimism that would somehow manage to seep into my DNA. For grownups like my parents, the joy of spring was welcome relief from the steel-gray determination of a long, hard-fought war. Painful memories were beginning to soften and fade away as the World War II years lost their sharp edges. As shed-blood scarlet morphed into sepia tones, a prosperous new chapter emerged, waiting to be written. Everywhere one looked, vibrant green shades of emerging life promised sunny days ahead.

I was too young to understand the collective exhale that Seattle heaved, but even at three the feeling of anticipatory joy permeated my awareness. Along with spring, Easter was coming, as sure as the flocks of robins that landed daily on the lawn fronting our red brick house on 31st Street. Spring was bringing pink blossoms to the hawthorn trees that lined the street. And it was bringing new clothes.

Ever since I had become aware of coats, a matter of mere months, I had worn a hand-me-down from my sister, Barbara, a cherubic, bigger-than-me elf with glossy black hair like Mama's and hazel eyes. She was one whole year my senior and I looked up to her as the epitome of wit and brains. She always made me laugh, and she knew how to read and spell. I had proudly worn my sister's old coat, a tattered navy blue, double-breasted affair, as a badge of big-girl maturity. Until, one day, it started to shrink, with fraying cuffs inching up toward the midway point between my wrists and elbows. The armholes moved up too, biting into my armpits and freezing my arms outward into a 90-degree angle position.

Even though climbing on furniture was forbidden in our house, one Saturday morning Mama picked me up and let me stand on a chair in the dining room. She held a piece of tailor's chalk in her right hand while she draped a tape measure draped over her shoulders.

"We're going to play tailor," she explained as she threaded my arm into a coat sleeve, leaving me to puzzle over what a tailor could be. Together we put the rest of Barbara's old coat on me, and then she bent her head down and tried to button it across my chest. I was admiring shiny black curls on the very top of her head, now under my chin, and enjoying the scent of her Mèmoire Chérie when she gave up the struggle. There was no way that coat would close.

"Gosh, kid," she said, tilting her head up and looking thoughtful. "There's not enough material to fix this. I guess it's time for a new coat."

"I want a pink one," I said. I had a newfound interest in pretty clothes, and pink was my favorite color. Not the dull brownish-tinged pink of pencil erasers, but a saturated, clear pastel, like my Grandmother Johnston's gigantic cabbage roses. All of Grandma's flowers were pretty, but most especially her roses. Their flouncy exuberance expressed the exact sort of effortless grace and beauty which I felt, more than knew, my new coat should have.

"That *would* be pretty," Mama agreed as her hazel eyes looked directly into mine. "I'll see what I can do, but no promises. Okay? The stores don't have much in them these days."

In 1949, Seattle was a world away from the East Coast retail centers. Seattleites who wanted up-to-the-minute fashion had to hire a clever seamstress or be one. Back then it took forever for new styles to come to town, with fashions in Seattle stores lagging many months behind the East Coast. But that was only part of the story. Consumer goods everywhere were hard to come by because the country was in recovery mode after World War II. The economy was in the doldrums, but right on the verge of shifting from guns to butter and war to peacetime. Although consumer goods were in short supply, especially little pink coats for three-year-olds, I had yet to grasp the concept of lowering expectations.

Later that day, Mama, Barbara, and I sat around a table that was built into the breakfast nook and shopped in Sears Roebuck and Montgomery Ward catalogues for Easter outfits. I jabbed my chubby pointer finger at a page with pictures of smiling girls my age, who were wearing gray, beige, and navy blue springtime coats.

"These aren't pretty," I said. "I want a pink one."

Our breakfast nook was in a small alcove that stuck out from the back of the kitchen. Even on gray days it was a bright and cheerful place to be, with warm light streaming through two windows that somehow managed to capture Seattle's shy sun. A U-shaped banquette upholstered in red leatherette wrapped the table, and that was where Barb and I flanked Mama, plastering up to each of her sides as close as we could get, our heads craning up at the glossy images. Mama held up the catalogue so we could see it and turned the pages, while my twin brother, Joe, sat on a chair at the open end of the table playing with Matchbox cars and Tuppy, an over-laundered toy dog with lumpy stuffing.

"Watch out, Tuppy," he yelled, screeching like an engine pushed to its limit. "You'll hit that tree!" He held up Tuppy by the ear and studied him with a quizzical expression. "Sheesh! Who taught this guy how to drive?"

Our attention was focused on the catalogues. Joe's commentary was a buzz of background noise as we leafed through three or four pages of coats that were single-breasted, double-breasted, short, three-quarter, or full-length. Some even had epaulets. They were what Mama termed "smart." I had something different in mind. I wanted "pretty," not "smart."

I pointed to the catalogue and said, "None of those. I want a pink coat."

"I know you do," she explained, "but there aren't any pink coats in these catalogues. I'll see if I can find one in the stores downtown, but no promises, okay? We don't always get what we want. Do you understand?"

I said, "Okay," but only because I wanted to be agreeable. My three-year-old heart was telling my mind, *Mama will find my pink coat.*

"How about a pink *dress*?" Mama asked as she flipped to a section with smiling girls striking poses in dresses. "I think we can swing that."

Most of the dresses in the catalogue were variations of the same style with a natural waist and puffed short sleeves, but presented in different fabrics and colors, and trimmed with varying combinations of lace, tucking, smocking, and ruffles. At best I thought they were barely okay. Not a single one was my idea of pretty, in fluffy, frothy chiffon or silky taffeta that made a soft/crisp swishing sound when you walked. Since I did not want to disappoint Mama, or drag things on too long, I felt compelled to settle for the lesser of the ugly evils. It didn't really matter, I decided, because the dress would be covered up by my new coat. Then we turned to the pages for accessories, like gloves and purses, but especially hats.

Easter hats were important, and not just because they were in fashion. Catholic girls and women had to cover their heads in church. Every Sunday this sign of respect and piety would erupt in a riotous display with hats of every shape, size, and color imaginable, most covered with silk flowers. The Saxe Florist greenhouses down on 65th Street, where we bought all our flowers and plants, had fewer blooms and less color than High Mass at Assumption.

Mama turned past the pages with gloves and purses to a section with girls' accessories, and we started scanning for springtime hats, suitable for Easter.

"How about this one?" Mama asked, turning to Barb as she pointed to a hat with a too-shallow crown and a wide brim, made of white straw.

Barb craned her neck closer to the catalogue, with narrowed eyes focused in a show of serious concentration. A moment later she turned her head while shaking a curtain of black hair away from her eyes. "It looks like she has a plate on her head," she said. And she was right, it did look like a plate.

"Yeah, and you know what goes on plates." Joe piped up from the end of the table. "Liver and onions!" We squealed and giggled, and the three of us searched for more of the hidden hilarity waiting to be discovered in the catalogue pages.

"All right, you characters," Mama said, interrupting us. "Let's take a break and walk over to the grocery store. We can pick this up later."

* * *

It seemed that wherever we went, Mama knew someone. We had just walked into the neighborhood grocery store, when we heard, "Hi, Esther," coming from the produce aisle. It was Eleanor, one of Mama's many friends from church. She wore a red bandanna tied around the sides of her head, and a row of curlers peeked out from the top. She was sporting the late-1940s version of the Seattle grunge look, consisting of one of her husband's plaid Pendleton shirts over a white crepe blouse with a string of pearls, a black skirt, and white anklet socks under beige leather wedge heels that had cut-out toes. Stocking-clad toes peeked out through those little holes, but I decided not to ask why. Mama told me once that Eleanor was "an original" when I asked why her clothes were so funny. After she and Mama exchanged greetings, Eleanor looked down and greeted each of us kids.

"Hi, little Mimi," she said when she got to me, calling me by my nickname. "How are you? All ready for the Easter parade, sweetie?"

I didn't know what parades were, but I was certain of one thing. "I'm going to wear my new pink coat on Easter," I said.

"I can't wait to see it," she replied and turned to my mother. "Pink coat? How cute, Esther."

Then my mother said something to Eleanor that didn't make a lot of sense: "Ix-nay on the ink-pay oat-cay. Oh-nay ink-pay oats-cay or-fay imi-May."

* * *

Wednesday morning of Holy Week was quiet. It seemed like a regular day, except that Lent was almost over. In two days it would be Good Friday, an important day in the liturgy of the Catholic Church. Good Friday was in the top three of all the major feast days, along with Christmas and Easter. Although I didn't grasp its significance, it was as much a part of the environment as the air I was breathing, or the springtime rain in Seattle. Mama, who sang in the church choir, practiced sacred music around the house as she cleaned and cooked and puttered about doing Mama chores. Her singing alternated between Lenten songs she practiced for Good Friday, *sotto voce*, some with tremulous vibrations expressing sadness and grief, with the happier songs for Easter that were octaves higher and felt lighter than air. Latin strains of *Dextera Domini*, with words that I didn't understand, gave way to the joyful clarity of "Jerusalem, The Holy City." Mama would sing a verse:

> *Last night I lay a-sleeping,*
> *There came a dream so fair,*
> *I stood in old Jerusalem,*
> *Beside the Temple there.*
> *I heard the children singing,*
> *And ever as they sang,*
> *Methought the voice of angels*
> *From Heav'n in answer rang.*
> *Methought the voice of angels*
> *From Heav'n in answer rang.*

And we would try to sing the chorus with her, dropping off after the first line:

> *Jerusalem, Jerusalem,*
> *Lift up your gates and sing;*
> *Hosanna in the highest,*
> *Hosanna to your King.*

With Papa away at work as usual, what was a regular morning for us kids was anything but regular for Mama. While she practiced songs of the season for the upcoming church services, Mama was immersed in a frenzy of spring cleaning so the house would shine for Easter. She was busy with scrubbing, dusting, waxing, vacuuming, and window washing all over the house.

* * *

"You characters play quietly upstairs while I wax the floors down here, okay?" We nodded agreement and Mama pulled out an electric contraption she called the floor buffer. "I don't want you anywhere near this thing," she said as we headed up the stairs. "Somebody could get hurt."

Up in Joe's room we whispered to each other, in an unsustainable effort to be quiet. Barb sat on the edge of a chair dangling her legs as she gazed through the window that looked down onto 31st Street, one story below. She began swinging her legs back and forth, and then Joe and I, sitting on the edge of his bed, mirrored her actions, swinging our legs in unison.

"What should we do?" Barb said. She looked up through intelligent hazel eyes like Mama's, except that hers peered out from beneath shiny black bangs. It seemed that she was asking the sky instead of Joe and me. Outside was a typical spring day in Seattle where the marine cloud cover cast a glare but stopped short of suggesting that blue skies were on the way.

"Let's look in Mama's room and see if my new pink coat is in there," I suggested.

"That's a dumb idea," Barb said.

"Is *not*!" I huffed back.

Sensing a squall, Joe interjected, "I know!" as he began to jump up and down on his bed, soaring higher and jumping harder as he gained momentum. "Let's play circus!" Barb and I immediately joined him. "We're acrobats!" Joe shouted as we jumped up and down in unison.

Minutes later Mama shot through the door with a dark look on her face. "What are you doing?" she demanded. "It sounds like Bedlam up here."

"Bedlam on the Bed!" Joe said, still showing off his trampoline technique. "Look, Mama, we're acrobats. In the circus!"

"Stop!" Mama's hands came together, forming a T-shaped time-out chop. In addition to undergraduate degrees in mathematics and music, she had minored in art, as well as physical education at the University of Washington. She could referee the games that grownups played, like basketball, tennis, and volleyball, and now she was about to shut down our game of circus. "We don't mistreat furniture like that. This isn't a gym. It's your *room*, Joe." Her eyes rested on each of us as she said, "You can't act like a mob of wild monkeys in the house. *Capiche*?"

As we chorused, "yes," because we always answered Mama in unison, I realized that we had let Mama down. Our intentions had been so good. *Sometimes*, I thought, *being quiet is impossible.*

Mama moved over to Joe's bookcase, grabbing a pile of books, some paper, and crayons. "Each of you read a book. Sit quietly and enjoy the book, and then draw a picture or color in the coloring book. Please be quiet and let me work, or I'll have to get Mrs. Bassey in to watch you so I can get something done around here."

This shut us up fast. Mrs. Bassey, an enormous white-haired, child-hating harridan, was our least favorite babysitter. Although she never actually hit us, she would yell and threaten, and then go to sleep and snore. She never played with us, like the other babysitters. But Mama liked her because she was a retired nurse, and she didn't mind watching us on opera nights. We thought Mrs. Bassey was scary, and although we did what she said, we didn't like her at all. "Mrs. Bassey, big fat assey!" Joe started to chant.

"Joseph!" My mother's eyes widened in surprise. "Where did you learn to talk like that?"

"Nowhere, Mama. I made that up myself."

"I *never* want to hear you speak of an adult like that again."

"Yes, ma'am." Joe said, trying to be serious, but I knew Joe better than anyone else in the world, even Mama, and I could tell he was trying not to laugh.

Under threat of Mrs. Bassey coming over, we quieted down and Mama went downstairs to pick up where she'd left off. I opened a coloring book and chose a Crayola in a lovely shade of pink.

I had only begun to work on a picture of a little girl in a coat, which I imagined as myself in my new Easter coat, when things became very strange. The chair I was sitting on started to dance across the floor. It felt like it was taking me for a ride. I looked up, and everything was in motion: Picture frames clacked against the wall; toys slid back and forth on the floor; curtains danced; and the light fixture on the ceiling swung like the pendulum in Grandma Gregory's big clock. I was too startled to be frightened. More than anything, I wanted to make sense of what was happening.

We looked at one another, and I could see Barbara and Joe were as surprised as I was. Then Mama burst through the door with our jackets over one arm. She scooped Joe up with the other arm and said, "Barbara, take Mimi's hand and come with me. Do it now!" Her voice sounded low, level, and devoid of everything but serious intent, and I almost began to be afraid. I had never heard her speak like that before. Then her attitude must have transferred to me because I forgot to feel frightened. Instead, I became focused and very intent on the moment. As Barbara yanked my hand and began dragging me down stairs at an alarming rate, I did everything in my power to remain upright. I told myself that I would not fall. Short months earlier I had negotiated those stairs by surfing over their edges on my bottom with legs held out in front of me. Although walking down stairs vertically was a recently acquired skill, we were so close to Mama's heels that I knew she would catch me if I stumbled.

The stairs were moving as we lurched toward the ground floor, and I did my best to reach for the railing as we staggered from side to side and downward. We rushed through the kitchen and out the back door. The shaking had mostly subsided by the time Mama led us away from the house and to the edge of Johnny Bear's Woods, which we'd named after Joe's teddy bear.

"That was an earthquake," Mama said, putting jackets on us and tying a scratchy wool scarf around my head. Then she explained earthquakes to us, and told us that we had to stay outside until we knew it was safe.

"How long will that be?" Barb wanted to know as soon as Mama had zipped up her jacket and tweaked her cheek.

"Forty-five minutes after the shaking stops," she said.

Barb's eyes widened in a moment of panic. "Oh, no. Papa's all by himself at work! What about Papa?"

"Don't worry, honey," she said. "Papa's been in lots of earthquakes. We'll call him as soon as we can. Till then, you kids run along and play while I pull weeds."

"I'll help," I volunteered, and we knelt by a flower bed blooming with early forget-me-nots. "Look, Mama!" I pulled a single pink blossom out from among the blue ones and held it up to my mother. "Look, Mama!" I repeated. "This one is the color of my new coat."

Mama started to say something to me but Barb broke in with an invitation to play ring around the rosy. It wasn't quite noon yet, and dew drops, still on the lawn, left cold damp spots on my knees and the seat of my pants after we had all fallen down.

"Oooooh nooooo," I groaned. "I'm all wet." Wet pants were unsightly, undignified, and uncomfortable, but worst of all, they were for babies.

"Never you mind," Mama said. "We'll get you dried off just as soon as it's safe to go back in the house." We stayed outside until one o'clock, well past our regular lunch time. We were hungry, and everyone had a damp bottom from sitting on the grass, even Mama. But all of us came through the Seattle earthquake of 1949 unscathed. The worst part of my earthquake experience was being damp, but mostly it was a fun adventure. The next day we looked at pictures on the front of the newspaper. Entire buildings had collapsed into big piles of bricks that crushed cars and blocked streets. And eight people died in the earthquake—people who did not have my mother to keep them safe.

* * *

Four days after the Great Seattle Earthquake, Easter Sunday felt bright and new and hopeful. With wet winter giving way to full-blown spring, it was time to celebrate life. The hawthorn trees lining both sides of 31st Street were dressed for Easter with exuberant poufs of pink flowers in their hair. They reminded me of the sea of flowered hats that ladies wore at High Mass. After church, Papa hid eggs for us to hunt in the backyard under a sky papered with forget-me-not petals.

Earlier that morning, before Mass, before looking at the trees and the sky and hunting for Easter eggs in the backyard, things had not seemed so promising. We were minutes away from walking out the door for the eight o'clock Mass when I tried on my new coat on for the first time. Mama had called me into her room as she took a powdery blue bundle out of its box. *This must be for Joe*, I thought, because blue is a boy's color. *Why is she showing it to me?*

"Here, honey. Let's try it on," Mama said, shaking out the coat and holding the arms for me to slip into. "I know it's not exactly what you wanted, but it's a nice little coat."

I was speechless with shock as I surveyed the sartorial disaster. In an attempt to accommodate my wish, Mama had sewn new buttons on it. They were flat plastic discs in an orangey shade of pink, like the inside of Grandma Gregory's eye socket when she took her glass eye out. After speechlessly climbing into the new coat I looked down and fingered the button over my round tummy. Acute disappointment was morphing into rage. I was on the verge of unleashing a monsoon of tears, but I looked up and met Mama's eyes. I noticed the concerned expression on her face and kindness in her hazel eyes. She smiled, in an attempt to coax a smile from me, and I melted.

In that instant, I knew three things for sure: That was when I remembered how hard she had tried to find my pink coat. I knew she had saved me from the perils of the earthquake. I also knew that I loved her, and I didn't ever want to hurt or disappoint her. In those seconds I decided not to let go of the tantrum that was brewing when she showed me the new Easter coat. With that act of will, I had negotiated what was probably my first sentient compromise.

Where we go in life, how we learn, and maybe some of the things that happen to us, good and bad, start in our homes and with our parents, with things like pink coats and earthquakes. Of course, we're also born with certain predetermined abilities or tendencies that can never be altered. Perhaps like a particular fondness for pink coats.

John Grey

Waking in a Fishing Village

"Don't bother to look," I warn you.
You're a stretch of my arm away,
cresting the warmth of my blood.
The name of this place is meaningless.
And there'd be no morning hug
but for bodies with people in them.
My half-vision lights you lighter—
don't worry, I've no vested interest in reality.
Outside, an old and bitter sea wind roars.
But in here, dreams have turned away from nothingness.
They've fastened doors and windows.
Now they open up,
breathlessly include you.
I catch your arm.
I don't speak, feel no need to eat.
I breathe heavily because
I've been all night in breathless nowhere.
Suddenly, my lungs know better.

I'm in bed in our cottage.
Jackets in the closet,
zippers stare at me like cats' eyes.
Cheap framed prints look over me—
likewise, underwear in the drawer—
telephone, light switch,
ultimately streets and houses,
docks and boats—
a fishing village.
On a morning like this,
crooked cobblestone
clatters one life at a time,
any and all who've survived the night.
So who are we upon waking?
I pity the ones without you beside them.
You shine through the murk,
face swinging its lantern,
lips whistling old shanties,
The Dutchman is running.
The outside world's untenable.
There's a thick fog on the move
but a thin one where I lie.

Excerpts

Dean K. Miller

from *And Then I Smiled*

An Unnamed Memory

I read about an unnamed beach the other day, though I knew which one it was. Setting aside the present, I left the now and spiraled back to the moments in my past.

An angry sea lashed against the rocks and cliffs along the shore and the setting sun appeared unsure if it should hasten its descent amidst the fury. Then... a new day, the sea, and waves more gentle. Their fury dissipated, they caressed the coves and tidal pools that gave sanctuary to the creatures seeking refuge from yesterday's passing storm.

Another sunset provides a back drop as a younger me flies a kite in the off-shore breeze. It is a simpler time, with fewer responsibilities. My choice: to stay or go home. Deciding to stay meant another day to surf, another day to hike the rainforests, or another day to build sandcastles. It was my time to choose. Life held all its promises, but I was happier to push them toward the future.

Maybe I'd head into town, pointing my desires at the bakery which stood amidst the trinket shops along the main thoroughfare. The delicious aromas wafted down the narrow street, drawing me in like a moth to a porch light.

Fluttering around the display cases, I eyed the treats contained within. Finally, to avoid deciding, I chose several different selections.

Or maybe, on rare occasion, I'd pick just a single donut. Dipping it into a steaming mug of hot chocolate, I'd watch the rain beat against the window. Nearby trees slanted seaward, straining to hold their ground, defying the strong, onshore gusts. The ocean was dark and gray, barely visible through the falling drops.

Braving the storm I wander onto the sand. Finding the right spot, it was possible to taste both the salty mist from the sea and the fresh water of the rain as it soaked me from head to toe. In the background a lighthouse and fog horn worked in concert, adding a touch of dramatic atmosphere in their routines of guidance to safe passage.

It was there, amidst the chaos of weather and waves, I felt alive. It was there I found tranquility. It was there I would smile.

Table Settings of Caribbean Gray

Sitting on the patio of our hotel room, the bay before me was cast in low clouds spitting drizzle that obscured the jutting rocks in grey dreariness—it was 75 degrees. A definite change in the weather, indeed, but not in the temperature. Solitude was easily found on the beach; weather related I am sure. Did the changing conditions reflect an unseen change in me? I felt the same; though in this morning's prose my handwriting skittered across the page in smaller letters. Maybe, like my surroundings, I'd coiled in, snake-like. Was I waiting to strike?

Undisturbed, I waited. No need to exert energy, yet. The curtain of fog eased out to sea. It was an odd scene to observe. At the Oregon beaches of my youth, the weather and fog moved inland, delivering its life-sustaining water to the interior landscape. Life on this island often proposed an unexpected scenario.

Certainly a time of change, that's mirrored by transitional elements. Like the seasons, life fluctuations can be subtle, or as violent as a thunderstorm. If I choose to weather the storm, my mood could reflect the changes brought by the parting clouds and warming sun. Suddenly, the overcast lifted off of the bay. The foreboding sky released its oppressiveness. A sign maybe, that the obscurities in my life could clear out as well.

Pelicans arrived from an unknown hideaway and skimmed the small waves, looking for breakfast. They climbed steep and then at the apex of their ascent, made a sharp banking turn and plunged toward the water. A violent splash erupted as the birds dove into the depths. Returning to the surface, they pointed their bills skyward. With ungraceful nods they swallowed their meal.

The morning sun crested the small mountain top, scattering the tension of the earlier overcast. I uncoiled my emotions, eased from the chair, and bounded across the small stone path to the sandy shore. My feet depressed into the cool, wet grains. A small wave found the courage to venture forth, covering my toes. The wave receded and I was left alone: the sun on my shoulder, a clear blue sky above, and an ocean of dreams stretching to the horizon.

The Wall and the Sea

I sat on a log at the beach, spending twenty minutes in quiet contemplation. My thoughts came and went. The setting, serene and relaxing, allowed my mind to drift elsewhere.

I returned to the present moment, unaware of what pulled me back. I watched the waves break along a small river jetty and on the sand in front of me. Across the inlet, the surging ocean ran up against a cement wall, built to keep the higher land and small home from eroding into the sea. With each crashing wave, another small piece was worn away. In time, certainly decades, the wall will crumble and the home swallowed by the briny depths.

But the sea was not in a battle with the wall. The waves that appeared to be assaulting it had traveled hundreds of miles, searching their own path of least resistance. Today, that passage ended against the wall. The sea, knowing only its pure self, went as far as it could without fear, without hate, without malice. Upon reaching an abrupt end to its forward journey, it turned back on itself, neither loving nor hating the wall, only knowing its new direction, only knowing itself.

I thought of my present journey in life, over forty-five years in the making, and wondered what it would be like if I were more like the sea. That if along my path, as I encounter my "walls," could I behave in a similar fashion: without fear, without hate, without malice, and without attachment? Would I be able to accept the path of least resistance, not in the manner of giving in, but in the functionality of only doing what needs to be done? Could I move on without worry of winning or losing, of poverty or riches, or of acceptance or rejection?

The ocean waves were rejected by the wall, but they did not change themselves. They merely changed the direction in which they were traveling. As I got up to leave, I thought of this and smiled. Now I, too, have a new direction in my life; to proceed without fear. Upon meeting the walls, I will no longer try to break them down. I will simply change my direction without worry of changing myself.

The Fire Hopper

It's no secret: my soul rests most easily when I return to the beaches of my youth. It's been a year since I last touched the soft sands of both time and the universe. But our meeting again, like old friends, was comfortable and moving.

We sat by our fire on the beach, its warmth deterring the chill of the starlit sky. One hundred yards away, small waves tumbled in, hushed by the receding tide but still whispering of secrets held under water too long.

The four of us talked about today, wondered about tomorrow and wished the trip didn't have to end. It was the comfort of family and friends drawn together by fire to a time and place of eons long forgotten. How deep in the sand would we have to dig to find ourselves in that earlier time?

Then a wayward traveler stepped into our small circle; he called himself a fire-hopper. Travis said he wished to warm his bare feet, the night's cold having nestled into the grains under foot. We welcomed him and shared the usual small talk: where are you from, what do you do. Idle chat flowed easy with this unannounced stranger.

A break in the conversation stretched into an awkward silence. Most eyes were cast down to the flame and its phosphorescent coals. I looked up at our guest as he took a few drags from the cigarette he'd lit when he sat down. With each inhale he closed his eyes and drifted somewhere I could not comprehend. I could see the immense pleasure in his gesture and wondered how it moved him so.

A few words followed, then Travis said good-bye, leaving our circle and our fire. He walked fifty yards up the beach to the next flickering, orange-yellow beacon. No one at our site said much about him. He had come and gone without fanfare.

I watched him leave the other fire and walk back in the direction from where he had first come. He stopped, put on a long sleeve shirt, and then walked into the darkness and out of sight. A strange encounter, it would seem. I wondered about Travis. What was he really looking for? Should we have inquired of his ocean side quest? Maybe we were too taken aback from his sudden appearance. I pondered these thoughts, curiosity setting in. Had we squandered a chance of learning and knowing by not inquiring of his past? What was his story?

But his intrusion was not wasted. It made me think about my own story. Much had transpired during our few days of travel, a journey that brought me home to the beach. My thoughts drifted, my soul not yet responding. Time had come to take stock of myself.

I discovered pieces of my past, and of myself, that made more sense than much of what I thought was real. For over half a century, I've been writing my story, but I'm only now beginning to understand what is written there, and how I shall write it in the future.

I will never know Travis' story, but that doesn't matter. What really matters is that he opened up mine.

Reflections from Above

One evening near the end of vacation, I went down to the beach to do my Tai Chi routine. It was close to eight o'clock and the surrounding darkness was topped by patchy clouds. The ocean waves created the perfect rhythm for my practice.

At one point I looked up at the sky. The clouds had parted; above my left shoulder was the Big Dipper. Though hardly a momentous occasion, it was a moment that gently grasped my attention. I was over 3,000 miles from home, yet that same stellar formation would be viewable there as well.

At first, it seemed this might inspire a feeling of insignificance. I am small and the universe is big. What impact can I really have? What I felt instead, was not the perception of insignificance, but of the vastness of the universe around me. As I viewed the astral splendor above me, I thought how great it must be to be able to show an identical picture of its self, even though I had traveled so far.

I understood then that I was part of this universe not to be insignificant, but to be grand as well.

In each moment of life, we choose to be big or small. In that choosing, we create the splendor of the world around us. Though we did not make the original creation, we are free to "co-create" the next moment of grandeur in the universe around us.

Susan Vittitow Mark

Aladdin: Population 15

In a line: hotel, cafe, store,
20 miles to Belle Fourche,
25 to Hulett.

Cindy B's Cafe is filled
with bees that do not sting:
bees on pitchers, Teddy bees
a tin wreath of contented bees.

Early, café's not open yet.
She lets me in the side door.
I drink coffee at the high table
topped with multi-colored tiles.
Some patterned—I spot three salamanders,
one cacti offering shelter
to someone in serape and sombrero.

Bob the Builder hangs low on the wall,
face crayoned yellow, mostly inside the lines.
He looks up at a photo collage
of high school seniors and cats,
motorcycles, young families,
and a fake tombstone for "Lucky,
the last dog to shit on my lawn."

Through the cracked and black-taped window,
dawn strolls across the sand-brown hills
of late summer and drought.

Cindy mixes biscuit dough.
Clatter of cups and pans,
A refrigerator hum,
Water running:
A lullaby.

Saturday Breakfast
at the Cafe

There's no decaf here,
and a half-order of biscuits
is more than you can eat.

The next table: four ball caps,
An old straw hat, two hatless.
They talk chainsaws and guns.
One got an antelope and a deer.

Work clothes—jeans, flannel,
Warm shirts with Carhartt labels.
They drink giant, mismatched
mugs of coffee, wait for plates.

"Did you order, Dennis?"
"Yesterday."
"What'd you order?"
"Burnt toast."

Laughter. They're on to coal trains,
600 people laid off somewhere.

I grew up in a house of men like them:
Father, brothers hard-working
with hands both deft and rough.

I hear my family in their voices.
I long to sit at their table,
held safe in that solid world.

Hal O'Leary

On Looking Back at War

What testosterone teased teenager isn't out for all the excitement and adventure he can find? Thus it was that I, with millions of others from both sides, marched off to World War II, never questioning, always seeking the new and different. I found it. I found it in the form of training films designed to convince us that the 'Kraut' was something less than human and therefore killing it was okay. I found it in discipline for the sake of discipline. I found it in the ignorance of good-old-boys from the South who were still fighting the Civil War. I found it in a ridiculous recitation of "Ours is not to reason why" from "The Charge of the Light Brigade," by our Captain as we boarded the liberty ship *Marine Wolf* bound for the ETO. I found it in the incompetence that sent our howitzers on one ship to France while we went to England on another. I found it in the fact that while they were flying troops from the States to reinforce our besieged forces during the Battle of the Bulge, we were rested and wasted, sans howitzers, in Denbigh, North Wales. I found it in the ghost town of Thum, Germany, devoid of all life but for a lone cat, which one of our sharp-shooters shot for sport. I found it in the rubble of what once were cities. I found it in the insane cruelty of Belgian resistance fighters attached to our outfit seeking vengeance. I found it in the grave registration "meat wagons" that passed us daily, with rigid arms and legs protruding from the overloaded vehicles. I found it in the liberated labor and concentration camps. I found it in the snow, the mud, the rain and K rations, in one of Patton's famed spear-heads. I found it in the plight of the German soldiers pleading to be captured lest they be taken by the Russians. Such was the excitement and adventure I sought.

There was, however, one adventure that proved to be rewarding. With the cessation of hostilities there came to our outfit a German soldier, looking for something to eat and wishing to be taken prisoner. He had discarded his uniform, and he, like so many others, was desperately trying to avoid capture by the Russians. His name was Albert Alfred Rupee, and when he volunteered to work for his fare, our mess sergeant was only too happy to oblige. So industrious was Albert that in the following days he made himself almost indispensable. He would do anything asked of him by any member of the battery. I soon noticed that the demands on his time became more than he could handle. On one occasion I, as a corporal, intervened when a private insisted that Albert shine his boots. With a goodly portion of the battery assembled, I informed the private, et al., that Albert was to be no valet to a hundred men and that his duties would be defined by the mess sergeant only.

This incident endeared me to Albert and as time passed, we became close friends. He told me of his wartime experiences. He was born in the Alsace Lorraine of a German mother and a French father. When the Germans invaded, they determined that Albert and all his age were eligible for military service, and Albert was assigned to the German navy. He hadn't been on his ship long until SS officers came aboard and asked for volunteers for the Eastern (Russian) front. Although Albert did not volunteer, he was chosen, and off he went to what was to become a most horrible fate as an infantryman in the frigid climes of the Soviet Union. He would describe how, with inadequate ammunition, the German soldier was required to rise from his foxhole and take careful aim before firing, in an effort to conserve ammunition. This would, however, expose him to fire from the enemy, who would simply raise his rifle from the foxhole and fire indiscriminately in all directions. On one such occasion, Albert lost three fingers of his right hand, but rather than relieving him, he was patched up in a field hospital and returned to duty. With the rapid Russian advance, the Germans found themselves in such disarray that Albert was able to simply abandon his company and his uniform and make his way westward so that with the ending of hostilities he found himself near where we were billeted.

Shortly after VE Day our battalion was deactivated and the cadre of non-coms that had come from the old New York 69th Division in Hawaii to train us had enough service points to be immediately sent home, and I, along with all the other corporals, was made sergeant to fill the vacancies. This made it possible for Albert to be retained as well. As Troops of Occupation, we were moved from town to town and upon arrival at each one, it became Albert's duty to reconnoiter for any loose wine and/or women.

Speaking German, French, and Italian fluently, and not at all unattractive, he became adept at this rather onerous charge. This, of course, only served to draw us closer together, and by the time I was to be finally sent home in May of 1946, our friendship was well established. A month or so after coming home, I did receive one letter from Albert. It was very brief and in the best broken English and German he or I could muster, he said that with my departure, things were not the same and that he felt it was time for him to move on. I tried to respond, obviously with no luck. Did he return home? It was then, for the first time I could remember, it occurred to me that he had never once mentioned his family or home after telling me of his parents' ethnicity. Whether there may have been some animosity between a German mother and a French father, I had never asked, and I had no reason to speculate.

I write this now in the hope that it may help you the reader understand the idiocy of war, for it is entirely conceivable that I could have killed my friend Albert, or he could have killed me. It is entirely conceivable that those we must have killed had the same longings for life and loved ones that we had. I was asked once by a friend, who became a super patriot after having lost a son to war, if I would record a research paper his wife had prepared for a national organization he had launched to foster support for the troops fighting the same war in which his son was killed,

Vietnam. In the paper, she accounted for every penny America had spent on war, and called on others to be prepared to make the sacrifice they had made in the cause of "freedom." I had to refuse my friend of course, and when he asked if I had a problem with his wife's figures, I told him I didn't, but I couldn't help but wonder what happened to all that money. It had to go somewhere. Who wound up with it? I told him that in his particular case it wound up in the pockets of those who took us to war with the lie of the Gulf of Tonkin. But sorry to say, there was no call in his wife's paper for them to make any sacrifice at all. Our friendship ended. I would, therefore, advise the young seeking excitement and adventure with my following fibonacci poem:

> Don't go.
> They lie.
> You must know,
> War is all a scam
> The rich get rich, but you must die.

Joan McNerney

Maintenance Man

Everything falls apart,
all things rot and crack.

Each day another tenant
fills out forms to request
repairs. Hot water tanks
burst, sinks back up, toilets jam.
Smoke alarms break.
It's a messy life, he pushes
against riptide.

All spring and summer,
weeds keep growing.
Leaves gather during fall.
In winter time, ice
covers walkways.

It's time to go home now.
Tomorrow he will return
to pick up the pieces again.

Tobi Alfier

Carolyn, the Apple of Avenue F

A childhood so consumed with painful shyness
she told everyone to call her Nancy. Even on vacation
her parents called her that, glancing sideways at each other,
shrugging their shoulders. Now blossomed and respected
as the one who gets things done she is reborn.

Her lover, skilled at making her know beauty and fixing
plumbing, has endeared her to her tenants. She puts on soup,
he fixes the sink in 2B, they make love and feast
like peasants. Innocent flirting has the gardener
water the walks and plant flowers for all seasons

out of gratitude for her sweetness and his visibility
to someone besides his children. She welcomes
the "hello's", loves chatting with the mailman
and baking cakes for birthdays and celebrations.
She speaks gently to the little girl in 4C, petrified

and chubby, forced into pink tights, black leotard
and ballet by a mother who cannot accept her baby
as anything but perfect. Graceful and grown, she tells
the girl when the time is right to be seen it will happen.
Don't bake the sweets until you're ready to be thanked.

Wisdom and Water

She closes her jet lagged eyes,
vertigo rocks her gently to dream-riddled
sleep of lichened boats, horses, and music
playing in soft language she can't pronounce.

Hilly, rocky land slopes to the movement
of ancient growth of islands, green and gray
sandwiched between the two blues
of sky and sea.

And in the farthest reaches of her dream,
a fisherman—a face familiar as time
but she does not know him. He is her father,
her brother, her lover. He provides. She sleeps.

Shadow and Quay

A rare morning—
the remnants of moon cross-hatch the pillow
on which her husband sleeps. She listens for the calm breath
that means he is traveling somewhere lovely in dream.
She touches his hand, he holds hers instinctively.

An unusual May dawn, the breeze floats through curtains
open to the peaceful day. She smells hearth smoke
rising from her neighbor's house, hears the morning birds—
the far off sound of steady song, a mockingbird nearby,
and always, the sea.

Soon she will know the place on the quay that scents
of rusted anchorage. She will watch the shadow
of storms against roughened plaster, she will see
the metronome ticking out the rhythm to a Celtic fiddle song
but she will not hear any of it.

And so this dawn, she memorizes her peaceful man,
imagines where the birds have lead him. She quiets
and treasures her own breath, where breath and heart
form a chapel. Where the music of remembrance is made,
where it will never be forgotten.

Anne Britting Oleson

Light

Cloudy all day.
Dark, agonizing sky.
Discontent rumbles mountains.

Sharp wind,
like needles,
like heartbreak.

No words
to shape
this angry desire—

until sunset:
a bloody blade
of light cleaves

like the single flash
at last,
of your eyes.

Safe

The way the storm windows
rattle in their frames when the wind
hurls itself at them—as they
have been doing for decades.

The way, in the corner bedroom,
the walls glowing with
the yellow of false sunlight,
graceful ferns of frost grow
overnight on those windows,
obscuring the snowy dawn.

Did that snow fall overnight?
You don't remember listening
in the dark, burrowing deeper
under the paisley duvet, but here
you awaken this morning, safe,
as generations have awakened, safe,
hearing the frustrated roar of wind,
against which the old farmhouse
cracks and groans, but stands firm.

Skinny Girls

I live in a third-floor walkup, on the edge of San Francisco's Chinatown. On foggy mornings, I sit at my window and check out the girls on the sidewalks below— Asians with cropped black hair that looks like a nun's headpiece, white chicks with knapsacks and crinkled hippie curls, and black babes who walk with a certain swagger. They all pass my apartment on their way to the Financial District, the Embarcadero, or to catch a bus down peninsula to some high-tech gig in what's left of Silicon Valley.

But it's the skinny Asians that catch my eye. I used to think I ogled them because of the year I worked as a cub reporter in downtown Saigon, where the taxi girls looked half-French and had attitudes to prove it. But I realized that I could trace my . . . my fascination . . . my obsession all the way back to Akela and the time we spent together in Sister Agnes Saint Jude's eighth grade class. It's easy for me to blame that girl for everything. But the truth is, I probably would have turned out this way whether I'd known her or not.

Part Chinese, part Hawaiian, Akela transferred to Our Lady of Sorrows Catholic School in the autumn of 1958. Her father had taught at the University of Hawaii before moving his wife and only daughter to San Francisco after landing a hush-

hush job at the Presidio. At first, I ignored Akela, especially during her first week in school, before she got her proper uniform. She wore classic pigtails that dangled to her waist. Huge flat-lensed glasses made her eyes look tiny and she always seemed to be polishing them with a handkerchief. She sat next to me at the back of Sister Agnes's class, near the steam heat radiators. I figured that coming from Hawaii, she'd need help getting used to the City's damp cold.

By the second week she began asking me questions about homework. I guess she thought I looked dorky enough to be a good student.

"So have you, ya know, made any friends yet?" I asked her at lunch break.

Akela frowned and stared across the schoolyard and the foggy bay toward Alcatraz Prison. "Nah, I'm not really good at that."

"Me neither. You want some of this?" I offered her the candy bar that I had spent my lunch money to buy.

"No thanks. My mom says I gotta watch what I eat, 'cause my face will, ya know, break out."

"Yeah, my older brother's got these big ole zits and—"

I felt my ears grow hot. What was I thinking, talking to some strange girl about pimples. I kissed it off to her being kind of pretty, at least to me. While some girls in our class had grown boobs, Akela hadn't yet. Her school blazer hung straight down her front and slender yellow legs stuck out below her skirt, with feet wrapped in white bobby socks and Buster Brown shoes. The boys ignored her, going instead for the likes of Beverly Quebec with her blouse stretched tight over amazing tits. Beverly sat near me in class and if I was lucky, I got a peek at her white lace bra between her shirt buttons. Akela would jab me in the ribs and grin when she caught me staring.

On cold mornings Sister Aggie cranked up the heat and I'd fight off sleep through history and civics class. During lunches, I tried to get picked for basketball or baseball games—but I couldn't dribble worth beans and would drop any baseball hit my way. So I'd hang out on the bench under the stairs and watch my classmates hack their way up and down court. Akela would join me, bring her pink doodle-covered binder, and go over her notes from the morning classes. Easy to talk with, she thought most of our classmates acted like juvenile delinquents, chattered away about how she hoped it would get better in high school, then college.

Yikes, eighth grade and already thinking about college? We steered clear of boy-girl stuff, mostly because the guys already kidded me about Akela being my steady. Personally, I liked the idea, but had just made the transition between a boyhood distrust of girls and a teenager's lust for them. Girls seemed complex, mysterious, and often acted crazy, one minute giggling and the next minute sobbing. But Akela made it easy and we talked about everything—the friends she'd left behind in Oahu, my failure at any kind of sports, people in our class we wished we were and the ones we detested, cool cars, Elvis Presley, the strange idea behind being a nun. But after a while we didn't need to talk, just sat next to each other and watched the schoolyard erupt around us.

One blustery lunch hour, I slipped back inside the school to grab my jacket from the cloakroom. To save money, the nuns turned off the lights in the hallways between classes and during lunch and recess. Near the dark end of the hall, a short line of boys from my class stood outside the janitor's room.

"What's goin' on?" I asked.

Donny Bruno glared at me. "Shush, keep quiet or Sister Aggie will hear."

The boys jigged nervously, hands stuffed into their salt-and-pepper cords. A giggle sounded from inside the janitor's closet. The door opened and Steve Sutfin slipped out, grinning.

He saw me and glowered. "What are *you* doin' here, nimrod?"

"I don' know. Nobody's told me what's up."

"Stand here and you'll find out."

He shoved me to the front of the line and the rest of the guys grinned and let me cut in front of them. They pushed me forward. I opened the door and stepped into the tiny closet-like room full of mop handles and toilet paper and lit by a dangling light bulb. Beverly Quebec leaned against the wall, her blouse unbuttoned, her skirt pulled down below her panties.

"Who the hell let *you* in?" she demanded.

"I . . . I . . . they just told me to—"

"Say, you're the creep that keeps staring at me." She frowned and stepped toward me.

"I . . . I didn't mean nothin', honest."

"Get lost, cootie boy." She hauled off and smacked me across the face.

I turned and bolted through the door and ran down the hall. My rubber-soled shoes squeaked on the polished Terrazzo, but not loud enough to blot out the snickering from my classmates.

Outside the cold air chilled me and I remembered why I'd gone inside. But I'd be damned if I'd ever show my face in there again. I sat next to Akela on our bench, folded my arms, and shivered.

"Weren't you gonna get your jacket?" she asked casually, "and why's your cheek all red?"

"None of your business."

She gave me a smirking smile. "I thought maybe you got snagged by Beverly in the janitor's closet."

"What are you talking about?" I protested.

"Ah, come on. You don't need to pretend. I saw those boys in the hall. It's pretty obvious."

"Well, it sure wasn't to me."

"Why? What did they do to you?"

"They pushed me into the closet . . . and . . . and—"

"Did you see anything?"

"Jeez, what kinda question is that?"

"Well, in class you keep staring at Beverly's chest. My guess is that if you got her alone, you'd do more than pass her a note."

I gave Akela a push and she giggled. We sat in silence for a few minutes with our backs against the school building, watching mobs of screaming kids race around the yard. I tried to scrub Beverly's image from my mind, but failed.

"Do all the girls know about, ah, Beverly, I mean, about what she's up to?"

Akela looked at me and rolled her eyes. "I may not be stacked, but I hear stuff. Don't the boys talk about girls all the time?"

"If they do, they shut up when I'm around."

"Ah, come on, not even when you're in the john?"

I felt my face burn and knew that no good would come from that conversation, that I was in way over my head, that if I tried to wise-crack my way out of it, I'd somehow confirm my status as a first class idiot.

"I didn't see nothin', okay?"

"Hey, you don't have to yell."

"Sorry," I muttered.

"I just don't get it," Akela said and smoothed her skirt over her tiny knees. "What's the big deal about bodies? The ancient Hawaiians, ya know, showed off what they had, were proud, I mean . . ."

I scowled. "Didn't the priests or nuns ever talk to the girls about, ya know, impure thoughts and deeds?" I had a sudden fear that only boys got the stern lecture and that now I'd have to explain it to Akela.

But she just grinned. "Do you believe everything those old men tell you?"

"Well, yeah, I mean—"

"Do you think it's natural that they don't, ya know, get married?"

I shrugged. Again, another subject I'd never really thought about. But at least the conversation had shifted away from bodies and I breathed easier. Then she unloaded on me.

"Do you wanna see girls, ya know, almost naked?"

"What? What are you talking about?"

"You heard me."

I stared at her unsmiling face. "I . . . I guess . . . sure . . . yeah."

"Come on." She jumped up and stood before me with her hands on her hips. "I've got something to show you."

She took my hand and led me up the metal fire escape stairs that connected to the school's second floor. We stopped at the top landing and looked down onto the roof of the girls' lavatory, a square structure with a parapet wall that bordered it. She pointed at two pup tent–shaped skylights.

"See those windows in the roof?"

"Yeah."

"The far one has a piece of glass broken out of it. It's right above the, ya know, stalls. If you look inside you'll see plenty."

"I don't know," I said. "What if somebody comes, I mean, they could—"

"Nobody's gonna come, and we still got lots of time until class."

"But . . . but how do I get down?"

Akela pointed to a drainpipe. "You can shinny down there."

"I don't know. Looks kinda tough."

"Ah, come on. If I can do it, so can you."

"You've been down there?" My mouth must have dropped open because she cut loose with a high giggle.

"Sure, the boys' bathroom is right next door . . . and it's got a broken window too. Busted it myself."

I looked at Akela and she stared into my face, laughing. I think I always knew that when it came to smarts and maturity, the girls had us guys beat. But a skinny girl like Akela being downright naughty?

She pushed me toward the railing where the drainpipe dropped to the bathroom roof. I hustled over it and inched my way downward, knowing that the climb back would be difficult. I glanced up at the fire escape landing. Akela had vanished. Oh great, talk me into something stupid then ditch me. I felt like I was back in front of the line of boys, being shoved into the closet with Beverly Quebec. But I had made it to the roof and if I was going to burn in hell for that sin, I might as well enjoy it.

I hustled to the far skylight and circled it, looking for the hole. The upper part of a large pane of thick frosted glass near the ridgeline had broken out. I heard the girls chattering inside. I lay flat against the skylight, my belly pressed to the warm glass, and inched my way upward until I could look inside. Restroom odors wafted up to meet me. Mostly little girls crowded the lavatory, but some seventh or eighth graders combed their hair at the mirrors. I stared directly below at a dark haired girl sitting on the toilet, her panties around her ankles. As I watched, she leaned back, her blouse pulled wide open. Akela smiled up at me and waved. She giggled and slid a hand down her front slowly, past tiny mounded breasts with plum-colored nipples, toward a triangle of black hair.

I stopped breathing. The blood throbbed at my temples. The chatter faded, then a loud crack—like the sound made when taking ice cubes out of a tray—and I fell, fell in a rainstorm of beaded glass. Screams, one of them my own. I twisted my body to avoid hitting Akela and caught a leg on the top of the partition. Then blackness.

Eight pain-filled weeks later, I left the hospital, my left leg pinned at four places, the knee shattered and frozen stiff. I walked like the character Chester in the TV western *Gun Smoke*. Akela's mother had phoned and told my mom that Akela hadn't been hurt but to keep her pervert son away. I finished the term at Golden Gate Junior High and attended public schools thereafter.

At first, after my expulsion, I thought about grabbing a cross-town bus and sneaking onto the schoolyard at lunchtime to be with Akela. But I had new bullies to contend with at Golden Gate, and new girls to lust after. Time passed and I never saw her again.

The bells at Saint Boniface clamor, bring me back to my refuge above Chinatown. The traffic of girls on the sidewalks below has slacked off. But I pour myself another cup of morning coffee and continue my stakeout, waiting for just one of the slender dark-haired beauties to turn, smile up at me, and wave. It's probably too late . . . but this time, I'm ready.

Poetry

Art Heifetz

Ratings

After searching for a mattress
on the web for over a month,
sifting through reviews and forums,
reading the litany of kudos and complaints,
he began to see his whole life
in terms of ratings.
He missed the five star romps
of his insouciant youth
and rated his present marriage
no better than a two,
three for ease of use and durability,
one for frequency of sex
and quality of conversation,
That placed him in the middle
of his age range,
which had a failure rate
nearly double that of their parents.
He fooled around with two girls on the side,

a four and five respectively,
but soon his wife got wind of it
and packed her bags,
taking with her the new bed and mattress
but leaving him the sofa to sleep on.
The sofa, alas, was like his marriage,
peeling at the edges and lacking support.
Only thirty percent of respondents
said they would buy it again.

Out of Sync

We are two watches
set for different time zones.
I steal across the bedroom like a thief
pants draped over my arm
shoes and socks in hand
while you sleep on.

I clean up after lunch
while you sit down for morning tea.
I soak up the tropical sun
while you hide under
two floppy hats
one inside the other
and hold a silver parasol
like a Victorian lady in Bombay.

You stay out of the water.
The one time you snorkeled
you almost drowned.
The mere mention of seafood
leaves red dots on your skin.
I glide like a dolphin
through the waves
and disdain red meat.

You believe in saints and angels.
You recite novenas to Mary
for all your sick friends
while I believe in
a vague spiritual force *out there*
or a God who lost all interest
millennia ago.

Yet for all that
our two hearts
have been in sync
since I first saw you
standing in the parlor
a timid schoolgirl in her fifties
not sure whether
she wanted to be kissed.

Richard Fein

Relaxing the Grammatical Rules of a Dying South American Language

The language is pronounced as trio. The spelling is uncertain.
The village is in Suriname.

Truth is a grammatical necessity in Trio.
The syntax of this language makes liars speak poorly,
for one must name the direct source for each quote.
So when a stranger entered the village and read
from the talking leaves wrapped in hides,
how the Great Shaman, Jesus,
commanded the tribe to follow the god of the strangers,
that stranger's sentence was grammatically incomplete.
For if the stranger was never eye-to-eye or ear-to-ear with that Great Shaman
how could he know what words the Shaman actually spoke?

In Trio the outcome of each verb is also part of its conjugation.
There are a half-dozen ways to qualify "to hope"
and a dozen ways to modify "to despair,"
but in their vocabulary of truths "to love" has no meaning.
for that infinitive, to love, is like a wide palm leaf that blocks the sun
and casts a penumbra that muddles clear distinctions.
In their tongue no one loves another,
rather they proclaim shades of affection.
One must speak this language meticulously,
for in this tongue hearsay is defined, lies exposed, and truths heard
in the myriad nuances of inflections.
Once upon a time truth and Trio were linguistic twins.
But enter gasoline generators, radios, and so many other fast-talking strangers.
Now when their grandparents try to teach them the old truths,
the grandchildren reply, "We're listening," but without a trace of inflection.

Ephemeral

adjective

1. lasting a very short time; short-lived; transitory: the ephemeral joys of childhood.

2. lasting but one day: an ephemeral flower.

noun

3. anything short-lived, as certain insects.

My father, my mother, the memory of their faces,

and mine also whenever I used to make childish mugs at a mirror,

now are like the faces of every stranger who ever passed me by.

I remember passersby briefly so briefly,

but now they've become barely recalled shadows.

My father, my mother, their precious faces

fade from my memory as my face is fading, even now,

from some stranger's memory.

Thousands of strangers have passed by me,

as I have passed by them

And probably none can recall the color of my eyes

or I the color of any of theirs.

Ephemeral? Yes, so are we all.

So how should I loiter through my nanosecond of eternity—

as a flower in its ephemeral splendor or as the short-lived insect devouring it?

Contributors

Tobi Alfier is a five-time Pushcart nominee and a Best of the Net nominee. Her seventh and latest chapbook is *The Coincidence of Castles* from Glass Lyre Press. Her collaborative full-length collection, *The Color of Forgiveness*, is available from Mojave River Press. She is the co-editor of *San Pedro River Review* (www.sprreview.com).

Pam Clements lives and writes in Albany, New York. Her poems have appeared in literary magazines such as *Kalliope, Pacific Review, The Baltimore Review, Earth's Daughters*, among others, and she is author of a book of poems, *Earth Science* (Troy Book Makers, 2013).

Tom Conlan lives, writes, and tends grape vines in the highlands of Northern Michigan. He has captained a Coast Guard Cutter, sailed the world's lakes and oceans, and fished the rivers and streams of North America. Tom's work appears in *Vine Leaves Literary Journal*, Issue #12, and he currently serves as nonfiction genre editor for *Qu, A Literary Journal*. Tom holds a Master of Fine Arts in Creative Writing from Queens University of Charlotte, and a Master of Science from the US Naval Postgraduate School in Monterrey, California.

William Doreski lives in Peterborough, New Hampshire, and teaches at Keene State College. His most recent book of poetry is *The Suburbs of Atlantis* (2013). He has published three critical studies, including *Robert Lowell's Shifting Colors*. His essays, poetry, fiction, and reviews have appeared in many journals.

Richard Fein was a finalist in the 2004 New York Center for Book Arts Chapbook Competition. A chapbook of his poems was published by Parallel Press (U. of Wisconsin, Madison). He has been published in many web and print journals such as *Cordite, Cortland Review, Reed, Southern Review, Roanoke Review, Green Silk Journal, Birmingham Poetry Review, Mississippi Review, Paris/atlantic, Canadian Dimension, Black Swan Review, Exquisite Corpse,* and many others.

Mitchell Krockmalnik Grabois has had over six hundred of his poems and fictions appear in literary magazines in the U.S. and abroad. He has been nominated for the Pushcart Prize for work published in 2012, 2013, and 2014. His novel, *Two-Headed Dog,* based on his work as a clinical psychologist in a state hospital, is available for Kindle and Nook, or as a print edition. He lives in Denver.

Rosemary Gregory is a graduate of Carlow University's MFA program where she specialized in creative nonfiction. With the program's Irish Connection, she studied both in Pittsburgh, PA, and in Dublin, Ireland, mentoring with Janice Eidus, Sean Hardie, Brian Leyden, and Leslie Rubinkowski. Gregory currently resides in Seattle and is working on a full-length memoir.

John Grey is an Australian-born poet. He's recently published in *Oyez Review, Rockhurst Review,* and *Spindrift* with work upcoming in *New Plains Review, Big Muddy Review, Willow Review,* and *Louisiana Literature.*

Art Heifetz teaches ESL in Richmond, Virginia. See polishedbrasspoems.com for more of his work.

Tyler Kline balances his time between working on an organic vegetable farm and studying English at the University of Delaware. A Pushcart Prize nominee, his work has appeared or is forthcoming in *Saint Katherine Review, 491 Magazine,* and *Forge Journal.*

Susan Vittitow Mark lives in Cheyenne and co-blogs Writing Wyoming. Her poetry has been published in *Sage Script* and the *High Plains Register*, and has been accepted by *The MacGuffin*. She is a past president of Wyoming Writers.

Jack Matthews, a previously unpublished writer, retired engineer, and professional curmudgeon, currently lives in Fort Collins, Colorado.

Joan McNerney's poetry has been included in numerous literary magazines such as *Camel Saloon, Seven Circle Press, Dinner with the Muse, Blueline, Spectrum*, three Bright Hill Anthologies, and several Kind of a Hurricane Publications. She has been nominated three times for Best of the Net and four of her books have been published by fine small literary presses.

Dean K. Miller is a freelance writer and professional member of Northern Colorado Writers. His work has appeared in *Chicken Soup for the Soul: Parenthood, TROUT* magazine, *Torrid Literature Journal*, and other literary magazines. He published *And Then I Smiled: Reflections on a Life Not Yet Complete, Echoes: Reflections Through Poetry and Verse*, and *The Odyssey of a Monk* (e-book short) via Hot Chocolate Press in 2014. His poetry and essays are scheduled to appear in five different publications in 2015.

Hal O'Leary is an 89-year-old veteran of WWII. With an Honorary Doctor of Humane Letters degree from West Liberty University and having been published in sixteen different countries, he has earned the right to speak out.

Anne Britting Oleson has been published widely on four continents. She earned her MFA at the Stonecoast program of USM. She has published two chapbooks, *The Church of St. Materiana* (2007) and *The Beauty of It* (2010). A third chapbook, *Planes and Trains and Automobiles*, is forthcoming from Portent Press (UK), and a novel, *The Book of the Mandolin Player*, is forthcoming from B Ink Publishing—both in 2015.

Terry Sanville lives in San Luis Obispo, California with his artist-poet wife (his in-house editor) and one skittery cat (his in-house critic). He writes full time, producing short stories, essays, poems, and novels. Since 2005, his short stories have been accepted by more than 190 literary and commercial journals, magazines, and anthologies including *The Potomac Review, The Bitter Oleander, Shenandoah*, and *Conclave: A Journal of Character*. He was nominated for a Pushcart Prize for his story "The Sweeper." Terry is a retired urban planner and an accomplished jazz and blues guitarist—who once played with a symphony orchestra backing up jazz legend George Shearing.

Harvey Schwartz learned Americana growing up on the East Coast. He unlearned it at Woodstock, a hippie commune, and during extensive hitchhiking. A long chiropractic career offered another perspective. He's been published in *The Sun, Clover*, and *Whatcom Writes*. Bellingham Repertory Dance and Snowdance Film Festival have featured his work.

Adam J. Sedia is an attorney who practices as a civil and appellate litigator in his native Northwest Indiana. In 2013, he self-published a volume of his poems, *The Spring's Autumn* (available on amazon.com).

Mike Sheedy's stories have appeared in various print magazines. Check out his bare-bones blog at mikesheedy.wordpress.com.

John Stack IV is a college student, develops hunting land with his father in Louisiana, and is compiling and editing a book of essays and conceits that he has written over the last several years, of which his "Confessions of a Southern Gentleman" are a taste.

Guy Traiber's writing has been rejected by many good and well-known publications. He will be happy to hear from you! Email at o13m@yahoo.com.

Stories That
Need to Be Told:
The Contest

Deadline: August 29, 2015

Instead of hosting separate contests each quarter for fiction, nonfiction, and poetry, we have taken a new direction.

Because TulipTree's mission is to help share your stories with the world, and because stories come in so many forms, we've created a new contest with only one category: the Story.

Whatever you call it (even poetry), as long as it tells a story, it fits.
There are no word limits.

Winners and honorable mentions will be published in a future issue of *TulipTree Review*, and all entries are considered for publication. The entry fee is $20 per entry. In addition to the cash prizes below, if your piece is published you will receive a 1-year subscription to *TulipTree Review*.

Cash Prizes:

1st: $1,000
2nd: $500
3rd: $250

www.tuliptreepub.com/contests.html

TulipTree Books

Available Now!

bigger
by Aaron Brown

Caleb Cross is worried his best friend, Bigger Falkirk, has lost more than his left nut after a tragic misadventure in South America. Since he got back, Bigger has been performing protests from a guide Caleb composed in high school. The guide contained a variety of recipes for sowing anarchy—recipes like the Pig Farm Prison Break and the Superstore Slash and Bash. They were all cock-sure, completely reckless, and written mainly to impress a girl. Now, however, Bigger and his gang of itinerant followers are causing major property damage and putting a great many lives at risk. Complicating things, forces seem to be driving Caleb and Bigger toward a destiny far stranger and more perplexing than either could imagine. Half-funny, half-tragic, *bigger* is a modern Orpheus tale about the perils of resurrecting abandoned dreams and the fierce magic lurking at the edges of our world.

Jake's Gift: The Story of a Cat Who Wouldn't Quit
by Pam Wolf

This is the story of one cat's journey from being rescued and then rejected, to becoming a therapy cat and television star and all the trials in between. Proceeds from the book will benefit the Fort Collins Cat Rescue and Spay/Neuter Clinic.

Call for Submissions

There's still time to submit your short fiction pieces for *My Favorite Apocalypse*—stories about life after your favorite version of the Apocalypse (we know you have one). Deadline: April 30. Details at www.tuliptreepub.com/calls-for-submissions.html.

Books to warm your heart,
nourish your soul and
spark your sense of adventure

 http://HotChocolatePress.com

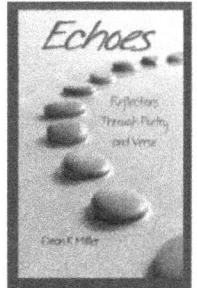

www.ingramcontent.com/pod-product-compliance
Lightning Source LLC
Chambersburg PA
CBHW081206170626
46811CB00011B/3329